Bem-vindo!

Imagine you have a close, personal friend in the Algarve, someone with the knowledge of a local, but also someone who speaks your language and has your special needs in mind. This friend will make it her business to entertain you, making sure you miss nothing the region has to offer in the days or weeks you have before you. She'll brief you on the fascinating history of this birthplace of seafarers and explorers, whisk you off to world's end for breakfast, guide you down to a deserted cove for a dip (with or without bathing suit), and then introduce you, by name, to the friendly Portuguese.

Susie Boulton, your friend and guide, worked for *Holiday Which?*, the leading British consumer magazine, for many years, and has compiled specialist reports on the hotels, restaurants and tourist facilities in the region. This research, combined with her long-standing family relationship with the Algarve, has enabled her to present this refreshingly new and authoritative guide.

This book consists of 19 itineraries which cover the whole of the Algarve, starting in the west and working through to the east. The Algarve is a very small, if extremely varied, region of Portugal, and any of these itineraries can be comfortably followed in a day. Susie has made no assumptions about where in the Algarve you may be based. In her experience, most visitors rent a rural villa, so she has planned the routes in such a way that they are all easily accessible from any point of departure in the area.

Take your pick among dinners of sardines or swordfish, deep sea fishing expeditions, mornings in museums and castles, bullfights, and nights on the coast. Susie's diverse suggestions will fill your stay with authentic Algarvian experiences, but they really represent just a starting point. There's always much more to discover down little used back roads and across windswept dunes. Like the Phoenicians, Romans and Moors, right down through the great discoverers, you'll be joining the illustrious ranks of Portuguese explorers, living out your own, personalized chapter of Algarvian history.

Bem-vindo! Welcome!

3

Insight Pocket Guide
aLGarve
First Edition

© **1991 APA Publications (HK) Ltd**

All Rights Reserved

Printed in Singapore by:
Höfer Press (Pte) Ltd.
Fax: 65-861 6438

ISBN 962-421-506-5

INSIGHT *Pocket* GUIDES

ALGARVE

Written by	**Susie Boulton**
Directed by	**Hans Höfer**
Design	**Gareth Walters**
Photography by	**Stuart Abraham**
Editor	**Elizabeth Boleman-Herring**

INSIGHT
pocket
GUIDES

C o n t e n t s

Maps

Editorial

Ich war zum erstenmal Mitte der 60er Jahre an der Algarve, zu einer Zeit, da die wenigen Briten, die hier Urlaub machten, tatsächlich noch „höchstes Interesse bei den Einheimischen" weckten. In meiner Familie gibt es einen Hang und eine Begabung zur Arbeit mit der Wünschelrute. Meine Großmutter und ein Onkel waren dauernd mit ihrer Gabel aus Haselnußholz unterwegs, um nach verborgenen Wasseradern zu „spüren". 1964 landeten sie tatsächlich einen großen Coup: sie fanden eine Quelle bei Albufeira, in einer Gegend, die so trocken war, daß dort noch wenige Jahre zuvor professionelle Wassserverkäufer ihre Ware literweise zu verkaufen pflegten. An dieser neuen Oase bauten sie einige Häuser – für lächerlich wenig Geld. Als sich die große Tourismus-Welle an der Küste ankündigte, verkauften sie und bauten sich eine Villa im stillen Hügelland von Monchique. Der atemberaubende Blick vom Gipfel des Fóia über grüne Hügel und Täler aufs ferne Meer hinaus ist meine früheste und tiefste Erinnerung an die Algarve.

Im Vergleich mit den Mittelmeerküsten mußte Südportugal zu jener Zeit als total abgeschieden und ursprünglich erscheinen. Die Frauen wuschen ihre Wäsche an den Flußufern, Ochsen zogen den Pflug über die ausgedörrten Felder, Karren mit Maultiergespannen waren ein vertrauter Anblick.

In den 70er Jahren kam der Tourismusboom. In der Zeit nach der Revolution war mit Geld nahezu alles zu machen, und Investoren mit den „richtigen Beziehungen" stiegen groß ins Geschäft ein. An der Küste schossen Feriendörfer aller Art aus dem Boden, vom billigen Touristensilo in Hochhausbauweise bis zu den ganz feinen Luxussiedlungen mit blendendweißen Villen am Rand – dank aufwendiger Beregnungsanlagen – smaragdgrüner Golfplätze.

Ein gewisses Maß an staatlicher Planung und Aufsicht hat manche schlimme Hochhausmonster an der Küste verhindert, aber der Bau-

und Immobilienboom hält doch unvermindert an. Die Algarve verändert sich schnell: immer neue Ferienorte entstehen, immer mehr alte Häuser und Korkeichen müssen gewinnbringenden Projekten weichen. Die Straßenmärkte verschwinden, Fisch ist fast Luxusware. Nächstes Jahr wird wieder ein neues Teilstück der Autobahn, die das Land von Norden nach Süden durchschneidet, fertiggestellt sein.

Zum Glück aber gibt es immer noch, unbemerkt vom Gros der Touristen und abseits der „erschlossenen" Gebiete, eine ganz andere Algarve: kleine Häfen, in denen Fischer wie eh und je am Ufer sitzen und ihre Netze ausbessern, ihre Boote streichen oder Fische ausnehmen, wo alte Frauen auf offener Straße Sardinen über dem Kohlenfeuer braten oder in schattigen Hauseingängen an den exquisiten Mustern von Spitzendecken häkeln.

Die große Trennungslinie der Algarve ist die EN 125, die Hauptverkehrsader der Region. Im Süden liegen die Seebäder, goldene Strände, Golfplätze und andere Sportanlagen, teure Bars und Restaurants. Das Land nördlich der Straße aber ist die eigentliche und echte Algarve: Dörfer, in denen die Zeit stillsteht, eng aneinandergedrängt die weißgekalkten, niedrigen Häuser, schmale, winklige Gassen, barocke Kirchlein, auf deren Türmen Störche nisten, winzige Bars (*tascas*) – zugleich meist Gemüseläden –, in denen zwischen Zwiebeln und Orangenkisten alte Männer vor ihrem Glas *medronho* dösen. Und überall grüne und blühende Pflanzen: in stehenden und hängenden Töpfen vor und an den Häusern, in Gärten und Innenhöfen. Die Dörfer sind umschlossen von Mandel- und Feigenbäumen, von Olivenhainen, auch Zitrusfrüchte werden angebaut.

Am Ende des Tages zieht es mich wieder ans Meer; aber weder zu der verbauten Ferienküste der Massentouristen noch zu den feinen Leuten, sondern zu den Stränden, wo man über Klippen klettern und einsame Buchten zum Baden finden kann und wo man fern vom Menschengetriebe am Meer den Sonnenuntergang genießen kann.

Die Algarve war immer schon eine Region, die vom Meer lebte. Von ihren Küsten stachen einst die großen Entdecker in See, die nach den Schätzen des Ostens suchten. Sardinen und Thunfisch machten diese Provinz reich. Auch heute noch kann man den Booten zuschauen, wenn sie zum Fischfang hinausfahren oder am frühen Morgen mit ihrer Beute heimkehren. Selbst in großen Touristenzentren wie Albufeira spielt die Fischerei immer noch eine bedeutende Rolle.

Daß Südportugal „Europas bestgehütetes Geheimnis" sei, wie der Slogan einst lautete, kann man heute wohl kaum mehr behaupten, aber es bleibt doch immer noch viel zu entdecken: Folgen Sie mir vom windgepeitschten Kap Sagres bis zu den beschaulichen Ufern des Guadiana, und sehen Sie selbst.

The Crescent and The Cross

Disembark from a boat and step into the streets of Olhão, and you might well assume you are in a Moorish town of North Africa. The windowless ground floors of the houses, the exterior staircases leading to the rooftops and the pierced chimneys are all eloquent evidence of the survival of Moorish ideas. Yet if you were dropped unsuspecting in the old town of Faro or in front of the cathedral at Silves, you would probably think you were in the mainstream of European Christian culture. This stark contrast illustrates the essence of the Algarve's history and culture. A Moorish province for over 500 years, it became part of Christian Europe while retaining its Moorish characteristics.

The Algarve has suffered destruction and decay countless times over the centuries. The sumptuous Moorish capital of Silves, then 'ten times more remarkable than Lisbon', fell into ruin after its final capture by the Christians in 1249. In 1587 (when Portugal was under Spanish rule), Sir Francis Drake attacked Lagos and sacked Sagres, devastating its oldest buildings; nine years later Faro was sacked by the Earl of Essex. But the most destructive forces of all have been earthquakes. By far the worst was the great quake of 1755. At 9.30 on the morning of All Saints' Day, when the churches and chapels of Lisbon were packed with local people at prayer, the tremors were so violent that the city rolled like a ship at sea,

12

Crusader, Silves castle

and houses cracked and split and, in a matter of minutes, the city was laid ruin. The resulting tidal wave was felt in England that afternoon and as far away as the Caribbean that evening. Much of what made up the Algarve was wiped out at a stroke.

What the earthquakes could never shatter, however, was southern Portugal's role as a seafaring nation. A province whose south-facing coast stretches for some 150km, its relationship with the sea has always been

Great quake of 1755

tightly woven into its history. The Algarve may not play a great role in world events today, but it was from here that the first explorers embarked on the daring voyages which led to the making of the Portuguese empire. For centuries fishing has been a major industry here, and fortunes have been made from tuna and sardines.

The first to take advantage of the abundance of the sea's harvest were the Phoenicians, who set up trading posts in the Algarve some 3,000 years ago and salt-cured sardines and tuna for export. The Celts, Greeks and Carthaginians all had brief spells of occupation but after the Second Punic War (202BC), the old province of Lusitania (roughly modern Portugal) was—despite stout resistance by the population under the much-sung shepherd hero, Viriatus, progressively brought under Rome's control. The best-preserved evidence of Rome's presence in the Algarve are the ruins of Milreu at Estói (Itinerary 13) where you can still see the remains and mosaics of a grandiose villa and baths, once thought to be part of Ossonoba, Roman Faro.

The Romans held sway until the early part of the 5th century. With the break-up of their empire in the west came the barbarian tribes. Suevi, Alans and Vandals swept over Lusitania, only to be extinguished in their turn by the Visigoths, who came as agents of the Romans and made their seat at the once Roman town of Ossonoba (Faro).

Moorish Domination

But it was the Moors who really left their mark on the Algarve. In AD711 they sailed from Ceuta, made a rapid advance and within three or four years had swept over a large part of the Iberian peninsula. Moors, mainly of Egyptian stock, soon colonized the Algarve and called it *Al-Gharb,* or 'land of the west'. New skills were brought to the land. Waterwheels were introduced, land was irrigated, rice was planted and almond trees and citrus fruits began to flourish. Craft industries prospered, and skilled artisans worked metal, leather and textiles. Christians had their own civil laws and lived cheek-by-jowl with the Moors. Some of those who worked the land continued to do so, but ceased to own it and paid rent to Moorish landlords.

The southern seat of the Moorish kingdom was Silves. It was a sumptuous stronghold with elegant bazaars, mosques, shipyards and a navigable port where ships loaded up with cork and citrus fruits. The castle is now no more than a noble shell. But as you approach the town from the south or east, through rich groves of

Moorish influenced tiles

fruit trees, and see the mighty walls and turrets crowning the town, you can easily understand why the Moorish rulers regarded this as their earthly paradise.

Apart from the castle, little else concrete survives to tell the tale of Moorish hegemony. But the dynamics are still there. Inland you can still see artisans hammering out copper and brass, craftsmen hand painting ceramics and old ladies working at lace, linen and embroidery. The most vivid Moorish architectural feature extant in the Algarve is the pierced chimney. Other Arabic features are the cubistic houses, interior courtyards and, particularly in the port of Olhão, exterior staircases leading to flat-topped roofs where fishermen's wives used to look out to sea on stormy days.

Christian Resistance

Despite the duration of the Moorish domination in the south, the Christian resistance began as early as 718 with a military victory at Covadonga in the small kingdom of the Asturias. But it was not until 1139, with Afonso Henriques' victory at Ourique, that any substantial headway was made. In the same year he became the first King of Portugal and, in 1147, seized the stronghold of Lisbon from the Moors with the help of north European crusaders. His successor, Sancho I, continued the anti-Muslim military campaign and began exerting pressure in the Algarve.

In 1189 Sancho persuaded some of the Christians making up the Third Crusade (with some English among them) to assist his fleet in expelling the Moors from Silves. They anchored off the city on the River Arade (then navigable), beseiged the fortress and forced the city to capitulate. The Moors, numbering about 30,000, fled and the Crusaders proceeded to loot and take booty despite Sancho's protests. The 'victory' is recalled today by the statue of Sancho in the castle, captioned 'King of Silves, the Algarve and Portugal'. Silves was recaptured by the Moors two years later but Sancho's successors, Afonso II and III, proved victorious. Tavira was taken in 1239 and Faro and Silves ten years later, at which time the Algarve became part of the nation of Portugal. Christianity took over but the spirit in which it is practised here today—with as much superstition as faith, and an abundance of lavish gilt statuary and carving—demonstrates a survival of the Arab mentality.

Following Moorish rule, the principal threat to Portugal and the Algarve was Castile. The climax of the conflict was the celebrated battle of Aljubarotta in 1385, when the Portuguese, under the then 'Defender of the Realm', João of the House of Aviz, crushed their adversary. The victor became King João I

AZULEJOS

It is thanks to the Moors that Portugal is so liberally endowed with glazed tiles, or *azulejos*. The name probably derives from the Arabic *Al Zulaicha*, or *Zuleija*, meaning ceramic mosaic. Other influences were painters from France, Italy and German and Portugal's maritime expansion.

Formerly a vogue among the affluent—there used to be a proverb to the effect that it was a a poor man who lived in a house without tiles—they are nowadays classless, decorating façades, seen on churches and chapels, villas and mansions, park benches and railway stations, and even the simplest dwellings.

Mass production began during the rebuilding of the country after the 1755 earthquake, happily, though, small family businesses, using old methods of tilemaking, still exist. The finest examples are in the church of São Lourenço, whose interior walls and dome are entirely faced with stunning blue and white tiles depicting scenes from the life of St Lawrence; the tiled stairways in the gardens of the villa at Estói and the Church of São Francisco in Faro with its scenes from the life of St Francis.

of Portugal and married Philippa of Lancaster, daughter of John of Gaunt. (Hence the foundation of the great Anglo-Portuguese alliance, the oldest in Europe, formalized by the Treaty of Windsor in 1386.) The royal couple's third son, Henry, would play a vital role in the history of the world.

Henry the Navigator and Manuel the Fortunate

Henry the Navigator was probably spurred on by mixed motives: love of Christ and love of commerce. At an early age he was appointed Master of the Order of Christ (the old Knights Templar), but most of all he is remembered as the catalyst for the great discoveries. In 1415, at the age of 21, Henry began to compaign for revenge against the Moors. He and his brother led a successful expedition to Ceuta, taking the city for the Portuguese crown. By 1427 Portuguese ships had landed in the Canaries and Azores. In the 1440s Henry was sending out the discoverers in new ships called caravels, powered by sail alone. Built and fitted out in Lagos, they sailed from there to the Cape Verde Islands and, according to Henry's will, 'into the land of Guinea three hundred leagues'. If this was the case, they had gone beyond the most

FISHING IN THE ALGARVE

As early as 1353 Edward III granted the fishermen of the Algarve rights by treaty to fish cod off the coast of England. At the turn of the 15th century the Corte Real brothers voyaged to Greenland, Newfoundland and Nova Scotia and, from then on, Portuguese ships began to harvest cod as far afield as Newfoundland. Dried salted cod became the staple dish and, despite the abundance of delicious fresh fish in local waters, remains one of the most popular Portuguese dishes.

By the 18th century the fishing industry was so well established that the dynamic Marquês de Pombal set up a chartered company to control the sardine and tuna fishing industries in the province. Vila Real de Santo António was constructed as a model fishing port.

The hunting of tuna fish is a centuries-old tradition, probably first introduced by the Sicilians and Genoese. Until relatively recently, the fish (weighing anything up to 450kg) were caught in nets, killed by a team of harpooners, gaffed and hoisted on board. The bloody battles that took place in the water between the tuna and the harpooners were aptly described as 'bullfights of the sea'. Today the methods have changed and tuna fishing takes place only on the high seas. Many of the fish, particularly the smaller ones, are eaten fresh, and others are preserved in vegetable oil and exported worldwide.

Fishing communities still thrive in the Algarve. Portimão is one of the world's most important towns for fish canning, though sadly you can no longer see the catch being offloaded at the quayside. The Maritime Museum in Faro is an absorbing place for anyone interested in the Algarve's fishing, past and present. For those who prefer a more lively manifestation, there are fishing trips for every variety, from the humble sardine to the dramatic mako shark.

Vasco de Gama

westerly point of what is now the African coast.

What Henry set in train was carried on carried on by Dias when he rounded the Cape of Good Hope in 1488, by Vasco da Gama when he discovered the East Indies in the late 1490s and by Cabral when, in 1500, he discovered Brazil, the 'jewel in the crown' of the Portuguese Empire.

When Manuel I came to the throne in 1495 he reaped the profits of those heady days of expansion. His ships brought back every kind of exotica known to the east and to Brazil, and the vessels were seen as the lifeblood of the nation. Conscious of the fact that he was the wealthiest ruler in Europe, he styled himself as 'Lord of the Navigation, Conquest and Commerce of Ethiopia, Arabia, Persia and India' and, for good reason, was nicknamed 'Manuel the Fortunate'. Architectural styles began to mirror the glorious maritime era and the king gave his name to the new movement, 'Manueline', a kind of maritime form, characterized by fine, often exuberant decoration inspired by nautical features, flora and fauna of the east, or legends brought back by the discoverers.

Fluctuating Fortunes

A little over half a century after Manuel's death, the nation suffered a devastating blow at the hands of King Sebastião. Having succeeded to the throne at a tender age, he turned out to be an arrogant and opiniated youth, convinced that his mission in life was to be some kind of 'Captain of Christ' against the infidels. Even as a teenager he attempted, unsuccessfully, to incite the Algarvian nobility to join in a crusade. But his opportunity came at last when the ruler of Fez was thrown out and appealed to him for help. He mustered a motley army, set sail from Lagos and landed at Arzila in North Africa. Four days later, on 4 August 1578 at Alcacer-Quibir, his hot and hungry men had no option but to join battle with a vastly stronger Moroccan force. In this 'Battle of the Three Kings' nearly 15,000 men were captured or killed and some 100 escaped.

With Sebastião perished the flower of the Portuguese aristocracy. The royal line was weakened and in 1580 the Spanish annexed the Portuguese crown. Sixty years of Spanish rule followed, during which period Sir Francis Drake attacked Lagos and sacked Sagres, destroying in the process the old house of Henry the Navigator,

and the Earl of Essex burned down Faro, having first seized the library of the Bishop, which he gave to Sir Thomas Bodley for the library he had founded in Oxford.

In 1640 the Braganza dynasty was established, bringing an end to Spanish rule. It was to last until 1910 when the Republic was founded. For a while Portugal was enriched by gold, spices and diamonds, debts were paid off and exuberant Baroque architecture flourished. In every town and village you still see the Baroque-style church, with its delicately sloping shoulders, vigorous doorway and picturesque belfry. The ornate figures may not appeal to northern European eyes, but are manifestations not only of a style of art but also a 'style' of faith.

Newfound fortunes and lavish Baroque architecture were devastated by the Great Earthquake in 1755 in which thousands died. In the wake of the disaster the already powerful Marquês de Pombal, Chief Minister to the Crown, gained almost total political control in Portugal. His methods were ruthless and arbitrary but, in the following 20 years or so, he did much to raise the country from ruins and modernize its industry. In the Algarve he rebuilt Vila Real de Santo António in five months and introduced state control of the fishing industry (later discontinued).

The Algarve, along with the rest of Portugal, was occupied by the French during the Peninsula War and Napoleon planned a Principality of the Algarve. But anti-French feeling was strong in the province and the popular risings in Olhão and Faro in June 1808 were some of the first in the peninsula. An assembly met in Faro and elected a kind of military junta of the Algarve. In 1808 a small group of intrepid fishermen from Olhão sailed in a small caïque across the Atlantic to Brazil to tell the exiled Portuguese king that Napoleon's troops had left his kingdom. Under Generals Beresford and Wellesley (later to become Duke of Wellington) British troops finally forced the French back into Spain in 1811.

Towards a Modern State

The second half of the 18th century saw the gradual rise of republican ideas in Portugal as a whole. Against this growing tide of feeling King Carlos I chose to govern by decree and was assassinated (along with his heir) by fanatics in 1908. Two years later the monarchy was overthrown in favour of a republic and King Manuel II fled to England where he later died.

The Republic failed to bring about popularly anticipated reforms and its life was characterized by strikes, economic problems and general discontent. In 1926 the constitution was suspended and a provisional government was formed. The next decades saw the dramatic rise to power of Dr Salazar, formerly Professor of Economics at Coimbra University. He progressed from Finance Minister to Prime Minister in 1932, and effectively ruled the country until he died in 1968. His monetarist policies brought about budgetary surpluses from 1928 to 1940 and his government saw the basis of Portugal's modern infrastructure.

Salazar was succeeded in 1968 by Marcelo Caetano, whose policies of liberalization caused serious discontent within the armed forces. This in turn led to the bloodless Carnation Revolution of 1974 (so-called because of the red carnations in the barrels of the soldiers' rifles). Elections a year later resulted in a an impressive socialist victory under Mario Soares. Since then Socialist or Social Democratic parties have been in power in Portugal and economic stability has always been of paramount importance to successive governments.

Geography

The Algarve stretches some 150km from the River Guadiana in the east, which forms a natural frontier with Spain, to Cape St Vincent in the far west. East of Faro the Sotavento is a flat stretch of coast with offshore islets and sandy beaches. To the west of the capital the coast is typified by cliffs and wide sandy beaches. West of Albufeira is the most varied stretch of coastline, with its weird-shaped rocks, grottoes, coves and promontories culminating in the barren and windswept Sagres peninsula, where turbulent seas crash against high cliffs. Behind the coast lies a parched-looking landscape of olive, almond and citrus trees. But only a short way inland it is surprisingly hilly. Eucalyptus, cork, carob, fig and citrus trees grow in abundance and hillsides are covered in rock roses and wild flowers. The Serra de Monchique, dividing the western part of the Algarve from the Alentejo, is green and hilly with wooded slopes and luxuriant vegetation.

CORK

Open any bottle wine and the chances are the cork comes from Portugal. Over half the world's supply is produced here and you won't have to drive far in the Algarve to spot the cork oak. The tree is easily recognised by its broad rounded head and glossy green holly-like leaves, or the raw red trunk where the bark has been stripped off. Cork oaks live for some 150 to 200 years and must mature for 25 years before the first stripping of the outer bark takes place. Each tree yields from 60 to 100 pounds of cork in one cutting. The layer gradually grows again and strippings then take place every nine years, the quality of the cork improving each year. Inland you can often see piles of cork by the roadside or large slabs piled high on carts or lorries, en route to one of the 600 cork factories in Portugal. The virgin cork is fit only for floors, floats or decorative purposes: the superior cork in your bottle will be from the second or subsequent strippings.

HISTORY

BC

1000–500 Phoenicians set up trading posts and colonies in the Algarve.

700 to 500 Celts settle and introduce the Iron Age.

202 Carthaginian Algarvian enclaves pass to the Romans after the Second Punic War.

202–137 Subjugation by the Romans and annexation of Lusitania (roughly modern Portugal).

AD

406–18 Barbarian tribes sweep over Iberia, including the Algarve.

418 Visigoths take Ossonoba (Faro).

469 Visigoths effectively establish their own kingdom in Portugal, including the Algarve.

711 Portugal invaded by Moors and quickly overrun. Last Visigothic military resistance at Merida (713) and Ossonoba taken in about 714.

8th century Relics of the 4th century martyr St Vincent brought to the sacred promontory of Cape St Vincent.

1064 County of Coimbra established by Ferdinand, Count of Castile.

1095 Afonso VI, now of Leon and Castile, entrusts his son-in-law, Henry of Burgundy, with enlarged County of Coimbra, now called 'Portucale'.

1114 Afonso Henriques declares an independent nation of Portugal from Minho to Modego, with Coimbra as the capital.

1147 Afonso and Crusaders conquer the Moorish stronghold of Lisbon.

1173 St Vincent's relics taken to Lisbon. Legend has it the boat bears a raven fore and aft which becomes the crest of Lisbon.

1185 Sancho I begins conquest of Moslem kingdom remaining in the south.

1189 Crusaders under Sancho I capture Silves. Sancho declared 'King of Portugal, Silves and the Algarve'.

1191 Silves recaptured by Moors from Africa.

1239 Christian forces enter Tavira.

1248 Afonso III, on succeeding to the Crown, musters forces for a campaign to take the Algarve.

1249 Faro and Silves taken—effectively the end of Moorish hegemony in the Algarve.

1385 Fernando I dies, ending the Burgundian dynasty. Juan I of Castile prepares to invade, whereupon João of the House of Aviz is appointed Defender of the Realm.

In the same year the Portuguese army under João of Aviz routs Castilians at the battle of Aljubarrota and João becomes King João I. He marries Philippa, daughter of John of Gaunt.

1386 The Treaty of Windsor formalizes the alliance between England and Portugal.

1415 Portuguese under Henry the Navigator take Ceuta. Beginning of Portuguese colonial expansion.

1488 Diaz rounds the Cape of Good Hope.

1495 Manuel I ascends to the throne.

1497–8 Vasco da Gama opens the sea routes to India.

1500 Cabral discovers Brazil and Spice Islands.

1520 Magellan sets out on his voyage to circumnavigate the globe.

1557 Sebastiao ascends to the throne.

1577 Seat of diocese of Algarve transferred from Silves to Faro.

1578 Sebastiao's crusade to Morocco and his defeat and death at the Battle of the Three Kings.

1580 Portugal, annexed by Philip II, becomes a Spanish province.

1587 Drake attacks the Algarve during Spanish War.

1596 English under Earl of Essex sack Faro.

1640 Spanish rule ended by nationalist revolution under the Duke of Braganca, later King João lV.

1662 Catherine of Braganca marries Charles II of England. Tangier and Bombay are part of her dowry.

1775 The Great Earthquake destroys Lisbon and much of the Algarve.

1807 Napoleonic forces under Junot enter Portugal and the royal family flee to Brazil in English ships.

1808 Peninsula War begins, Portuguese army supporting Wellington. 16 June civil uprising at Olhão followed by one at Faro setting up a Provincial Junta of the Algarve.

1810 Massena prevented from entering Lisbon by the lines of Torres Vedras.

1811 French leave Portugal.

1832–4 War of the Two Brothers, between Miguel (Liberals) and Pedro (Absolutists) for the Crown. Miguel's navy helped by the English off Cape St Vincent. Faro, a liberal headquarters, is beseiged by Absolutists.

1903 Treaty of Windsor publicly reaffirmed during a visit by Edward VII to Portugal.

1908 King Carlos assassinated by liberal fanatics.

1910 Portugal declared a republic. Manuel II is forced to abdicate and flees to England.

1926 Gomes da Costa dictatorship begins, followed by *coup d'etat* after which Carmona becomes president.

1928 After successive budgetary disasters, Salazar is appointed Minister of Finance to restore economic order.

1932 Salazar becomes prime minister, retaining financial portfolio.

1939–45 Portugal, while remaining neutral in the war, leases the Azores to the USA, thereby helping to break the German submarine campaign on Anglo-American shipping lines.

1968 Salazar dies and Caetano takes over and begins a policy of liberalization.

1974 MFA (Armed Forces Movement) overthrows government in a bloodless revolution. After independence, some 700,000 refugees from former colonies pour into Portugal.

1976 A constitution is drawn up based on universal suffrage and a single legislative chamber. Socialists win election and Dr Soares becomes prime minister of a minority government.

1986 Portugal becomes a member of the EEC.

1. World's End – The Sagres Peninsula

Salema beach for breakfast and morning dip; Sagres peninsula and Cape St Vincent; afternoon on an unspoilt beach.

No wonder this gaunt, windswept promontory was once known as the *Fim do Mundo*. Waves crash against giant cliffs, aloes bow to the winds and fig trees huddle against the barren land. Take the modern houses away and you can imagine why this southwestern tip of continental Europe was believed by the great discoverers to be the end of the world. It was here that the half-English Henry the Navigator mustered together the most famous cartographers, boat builders and mariners to plot the famous voyages which were to found the Portuguese Empire. In true Algarvian style, Sagres has a meagre supply of tourist information. Brush up on your history first if you want to get the most out of this major landmark.

Start the day on the sweeping beach at **Salema** with an early morning dip or gentle jog along the sands. Watch the fishermen drag the skiffs up the beach, lay out their morning's catch and wash squid on the sands. Stoke up on a cooked or continental breakfast at the Miramar beach bar (open from 9am), just off the narrow street of fishermen's houses running parallel to the beach. Sit on the bamboo terrace overlooking the sea.

By the time the tourists start to arrive on the beach (10–10.30am) you should be heading west. Join the main EN125 and turn left towards Sagres. Two kilometres after the village of Figueira look out on the right for the **Chapel of Guadalupe**, a delightful little church where Henry the Navigator used to pray for help on his planned routes to distant lands. He lived for a while at Raposeira, a dozy village further along the main road. See the house if you wish (ask at the café in the square for instructions), but it looks neither old nor remarkable.

Stop briefly at **Vila do Bispo** to admire the blue and gold extravaganza in the Baroque church. Ask the sacristan to switch on the lights so you can see the fine blue and white *azulejos* depicting a whole range of secular motifs, the painted wood ceiling and the chancel in gilded wood. Note as you come out the café Correia in the street roughly running opposite the church. Here barnacles (*percebes*) are the speciality.

Rejoin the main road which now runs over a windswept plateau where plants are sparse and trees are stunted. Drive through the straggling outskirts of Sagres, typified by squat road side homes advertising *quartos* (rooms). When you reach the town follow the sign for the **Fortaleza,** whose awesome walls will soon loom on the horizon. Drive over the narrow peninsula, through the tunnel-like fortified gateway, and park inside the fortress.

The original buildings and walls were destroyed and what is claimed to have been Henry's School of Navigation is now a youth hostel. Use your imagination to picture the great marine think tank and the caravels coming round the cape with their booty from distant lands. What may be original is the large *rosa do ventos*, a type of mariners' compass, which you can see on the left

Fishermen on Salema beach

as you come into the fortress. It was only discovered in 1928 and still looks somewhat weed infested and forgotten.

Take the track to the right, past the peeling white facade of the small domed chapel (where Henry probably worshipped) and follow the route skirting the edge of the cliffs. Go by foot if it's not too gusty and you have the stamina. Stop at the tip of the promontory near the red-topped lighthouse and watch weather-beaten fishermen, perched on precarious ledges, casting their lines into the rough seas below. Fish for dinner is taken home in wicker baskets lodged on the back of Vespas, with long rods towering above. Admire views (weather permitting) of the lighthouse at Cape of St Vincent to the west, the cliffs to the east as far as Lagos and out to the seemingly infinite ocean.

Get a better view of **Cape St Vincent** by taking the main EN268 westward. (The road is marked to the Cabo de San Vicente at the Sagres roundabout.) Drive over the wind-battered plateau for 6km. Before reaching the cape you'll see on the left the old fortress of Belixe, now a restaurant with four rooms and an old chapel. On arrival at the cape, park near the stalls selling fishermen's socks and chunky sweaters. The lighthouse sits at the tip of the promontory, surrounded by neat gardens and spectacular sea vistas. Watch ocean-going vessels rounding the cape from the lookout point to the right of the lighthouse and the sea breakers crashing into the grottoes of the cliffs 70m below. Visits inside the lighthouse are, it seems, entirely dependent on the mood of the keeper on duty. Try to join on the tail of a visiting group or, if the door to the lighthouse (at the end of the pathway) is shut, track down a keeper and try your powers of persuasion. The interior is fascinating: massive crystal, gleaming brass, 3,000 Watt bulbs. The lantern, de-

signed and made in France, is the biggest in Europe, with a light visible from a distance of 90kms.

Return to Sagres for a lobster lunch overlooking the port. At the main roundabout go straight ahead, then turn right when you see the Hotel Baleeira. This brings you down to the port and the **A Tasca Restaurant** (Tel: 082-64177) overlooking it. Converted from the old market it's full of character and has first-class fresh fish—much of it caught on the restaurant's own boat. (Opening hours 12pm–10pm, closed on Saturdays.) Specialities are lobster (8,500$ a kilo) and *amêijoas na cataplana* (clams in cataplana). Eat outside on the sea view terrace or in the large interior, complete with oven for smoking fish. Linger over lunch for as long as you wish. If a boat trip to see the coast and grottoes appeals, ask down at the port (or telephone in advance: 082-66271).

Spend what remains of the afternoon on a beach. To keep off the beaten track try the gorgeous **Praia do Zavial** on the south coast or, for a taste of the real Atlantic, the dramatic **Praia do Castelejo**, northwest of Vila do Bispo. For Zavial, return to Raposeira, take the right turn marked Ingrina and Hortas do Tabula, bump over the potholed track for 1km, fork left and the beach is 3km further on. For Praia do Castelejo return to Vila do Bispo and, just before the centre, turn left down the road marked Praia do Castelejo. A rough, narrow road winds through hills covered in cistus and brings you down to a sweeping beach, where Atlantic rollers break on golden sands. Brave the waters (but watch the currents), then take an evening drink on the panoramic terrace of the beach bar. On a warm evening this is a lovely spot to dine on *arroz de pesce* and watch the sun set.

The Fort at Sagres

2. Sun and Surf – Beaches Around Sagres

Leisurely breakfast at the pousada in Sagres; trip up the west coast, exploring unspoilt beaches; early evening at Aljezur; sunset from Cape St Vincent or Sagres.

Winds, waves and coolish waters keep the majority of holiday makers off the Algarve's west coast. What they miss is a series of wild, stunningly beautiful beaches, many reached only via dirt tracks or by foot.

Start the day in Sagres and treat yourself to breakfast at the **Pousada do Infante**. One of the only two state-sponsored hotels in the Algarve (and infinitely superior to the other), the Do Infante is stylish and civilised with lush lawns, spacious rooms and a prime cliff top location looking across the rugged coast to the *fortaleza*. Breakfast sets you back 900$ but is more ample than most.

Before leaving Sagres, watch some of the morning's fishing activity down at the **port** and **market** (turn right at the main road and right again at the Hotel Baleeira) and visit the **fortaleza** where Henry the Navigator is said to have set up his navigation school and plotted his great expeditions.

Leave Sagres by mid to late morning and make for the west coast via the small town of Vila do Bispo. Take the main EN268 out of Sagres and as you come into Vila do Bispo watch for the left turning marked to **Praia do Castelejo**. A rough, narrow road takes you to one of the more accessible beaches on the west coast, but no less beautiful for that. The sweeping sands, high cliffs and hinterland of hilly moors carpeted in wild flowers make a splendid sight. Brave the waves, walk the cliff tops or just sit at the beach bar terrace and admire the view.

Your next stop is **Carrapateira**, further north. The only way to get there is to return to Vila do Bispo, turn left onto the main EN125 and left again just after the village, marked to Aljezur. The road is potholed but traffic-free with wayside eucalyptus trees and pines arching over the road. The village of Carrapateira is little more than a jumble of houses on steep cobbled streets, a tiny marketplace and a handful of bars with resting backpackers and thirsty surfers. What really makes the place are the beaches. See them on a fine day and and it is hard to believe that such beauty spots, with their sweeps of sand, dramatic surf and cliffs are still undiscovered. The only people on the beach are likely to be a handful of surfers or latter day hippies soaking up the sun.

To get to the first beach, **Amado**, take the first turn left after the *Escola Primario* (primary school) which you see as you come into Carrapateira. The distance to the beach is about 2km, along a dirt track and through a national park. Pass the Pensão Valentin (nice rustic French-run B&B) after about 200m and follow the road until it reaches a fork where you bear left. This is where the spectacular views of cliffs and sea begin. About 250m before you come to the beach, watch out for a shack marked *Restaurante* and don't be deterred by shabby appearances. Manuel António's café has excellent grilled fish or chicken, good sea views and a very friendly atmosphere. Service is very laid back, so specify a time for your lunch, order it and come back later. Meanwhile, make the most of the beach, with its beautiful long stretch of unspoilt sand

and dunes. If you bathe, watch out for currents and sizable waves. Off season, walk along the cliffs for splendid sea views. In spring pretty wild flowers of all colours grow in the stony soil.

Don't leave Carrapateira without taking at least a brief look at the staggeringly beautiful beach of **Bordeira** a little further up. Go back to the main road, turn left and very soon left again, along another dusty dirt track. Drive for about 2km past dusty cacti and fig trees, where the washing is hung out to dry, and you will see down to your right a dramatic sweep of beach, dunes and cliffs. There are even better views if you drive a little way further up the hill, where a lone goatherd may be sitting on the cliffs with his brown-speckled goats.

Leave Carrapateira by late afternoon and rejoin the EN268 for the town of **Aljezur**. The road cuts inland, through deserted hilly territory to Alfambras. Ignore the road here to Lagos and go straight on to Aljezur, passing neat rows of vines as you go. When you get to the centre of the town, turn right over the bridge, park by the marketplace/tourist office, and make your way up by foot to the castle (see Itinerary 7). Dependent on the time and the whereabouts of your base, either take the main road south to Lagos or retrace your steps along the west coast to watch the sun sink at Cape St Vincent or Sagres. If you want to stay in the area for dinner try the excellent A Tasca Restaurant at Sagres port (see Itinerary 1) which is open until 8pm.

Previous page: Dona Ana beach;
Left: Lagos

3. Lagos and Dona Ana

A day in and around the city of Lagos: microlighting, sightseeing and browsing around the old town; early evening dip at Dona Ana and boat trip around the coves. (Microlights need to be reserved in advance: Tel: 082-62906.)

A major port and capital of the Algarve for two centuries, Lagos is historically one of the region's most interesting cities. Caravels sailed in here with slaves, ivory and gold; Dom Sebastião left from its shores on his disastrous mission to conquer Morocco, and Sir Frances Drake attacked the city in 1587. All this seems far removed from modern day Lagos, crammed with bars and restaurants that cater for all tastes and nationalities. Happily though, culture and tourism blend together. Despite earthquake devastation and, more recently, the concrete sprawl, there is still an elegance about the central streets and squares, and sufficient historical landmarks to ensure that the past survives.

For a bird's eye view of the whole bay, take to the skies in the **microlights** with long distance world record holders Gerry and Manueal Breen. The aerodrome lies on the main EN125 north of town, open 9am to 12pm. A seven-minute trip, at 6,500$ will take you round the bay, and 15-minute trips down to Burgau cost 9,000$ (no photos allowed).

Spend the rest of the morning in Lagos centre, starting at the main square, Praça Infante Dom Henrique, confusingly also called the Praça da República. In summer parking can be a problem and you may have to cruise up and down the harbour side road till you find a space.

From the square with its gardens and café you can pinpoint various historical landmarks. Look first at the large bronze statue of **Henry the Navigator**, appropriately looking seaward, sextant in hand. As governor he lived in the *Castelo dos Governadores* on the west side of the square. Facing the statue and to your left in the distance is the old fort which defended the entrance to the port in the 17th century. On the south side of the square the Church of Santa Maria is unremarkable apart from some good 18th-century wooden statuary. More or less opposite the insignificant arcade under the Lagos Customs House is the site of the **Mercado dos Escravos,** where the hapless African slaves used to be sold. Take the cobbled Rua Henrique Correia de Silva (near the church) up to the museum and **Chapel of Santo António**. The plain façade belies the most lavish ecclesiastical interior of the Algarve and one of the very few to survive the 1755 earthquake. The walls are almost entirely faced with intricately carved gilded woodwork. The entrance to the **Regional Museum** is on the right (open, like the church, 9am–12.30pm, 2pm–5pm, Monday and holidays excepted). The first section is devoted to archaeological finds from all over the Algarve; then there's a more extended ethnographic section with all things Algarvian: sardine nets, lobster pots, pierced chimneys, farming implements, plus some oddities preserved in bottles, such as a one-eyed sheep and two-headed cat. Labelling as usual is in Portuguese only but staff speak a smattering of English.

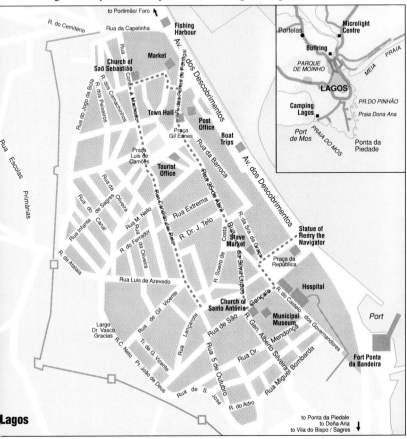

Lagos

Exiting the museum/church turn right, down the Rua da Silves Lopes, which leads into the hub of central Lagos: Rua 25 de Abril. Stop at **Casa do Papagaio**, Nos. 27 and 29, on your right where a couple of loquacious parrots catch the eye of passers-by and lure them into a dark and fascinating treasure trove of Portuguese antiques: everything from coins and cash tills to African statuary. Note almost opposite the **Restaurante Sebastião** (Tel: 082-62795), pricey by local standards but a favourite with foreigners for location, open air terrace and variety of food.

Fork left at the end of the street, past the tourist office and into

the Praça Gil Eanes, named after the first explorer to round Cape Bojador, a far-flung point on the west coast of the Sahara. Cross the square, casting a glance as you go at the provocative statue of the pink-faced Sebastião, a precocious 13-year-old. Carry on, past the gardens and post office on your right, and make for the fish and vegetable market which stands back from the main harbour side road. Just beyond the market there's a good *pastelaria* for fancy marzipan cakes.

Retrace your steps a little way until you see a flight of steps up to your right. Go to the top, turn right, then wind left and along to the **Church of São Sebastião.** Note the Renaissance portal and, if it happens to be open, the decorative tiles inside. Come down the steep Rua Conselheiro Joaquim Machado into the Praça Luís de Camões, named after the Portuguese poet. Spend any remaining time before lunch browsing in the Rua Cândido dos Reis, or explore some of the streets east, going up to the old city walls.

For lunch choose between Sebastião or for somewhere simpler, the **O Pescador** in Rua Gil Eanes (first street on the left as you came into the square). Alternatively pick a restaurant of your own choice.

Linger over lunch, then spend part of the afternoon browsing around **Lagos** at leisure (shops open at 3pm). By late afternoon make for the promontory south of the city where sandy coves and clear grottoes lie beneath weathered cliffs. Either take a boat from the waterfront (2,500$ per boat, 50-minute trip), weather and waves permitting, or drive to the tip of the promontory and get a cheaper trip there. Follow the main road towards Sagres, take the left turning marked for Dona Ana and Ponta da Piedade. At the first fork turn left and follow the road down to the lighthouse. Park the car, take the track to the left over the promontory for a

4. Portimão and Ferragudo

Portimão for morning shopping and sardine lunch; Praia da Rocha beach; Ferragudo for dinner.

For some time now major bridge and road construction has deterred tourists from going into the centre of Portimão. The estimated date for completion is 1992: until then be prepared for traffic jams and long diversions around the city.

The smell of sardines permeating street corners is a sure indication that this is an active fishing port. Until relatively recently, the key attraction for the tourist was the sight of the fresh fish tossed up in wicker baskets onto the quayside. For tax purposes, the landing of the fish now takes place in a closed-off area on the other side of the estuary. Now you are unlikely to see more than occasional smack coming in with sardines or a fishermen washing and slicing inky squid on the quayside.

On the plus side, Portimão has the best shopping in the Algarve and plenty of cheap places to eat fish. Sardines are at their fattest and best in July, August and September. Some of the locals won't touch them at other times of the year.

Park as near to the old fishing port as you can and browse around the **river quays** where cruisers and trawlers are usually an-

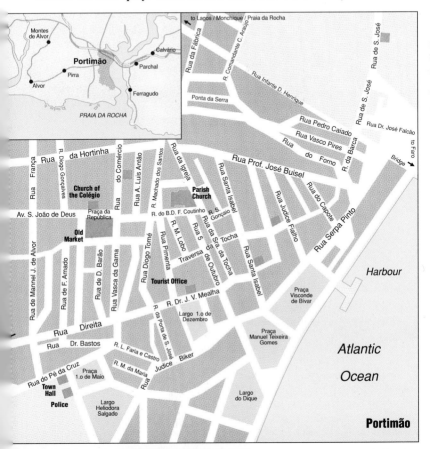

chored. Book now if you want a day's big game fishing (See Itinerary 5) or a day on a yacht sailing down the coast.

Stop for coffee in the **public gardens** nearby, then explore the old residential quarter by taking the narrow streets off the Rua Serpa Pinto. Spend the rest of the morning shopping, starting with the **Rua Santa Isabel** where up-market shops occupy the ground floors of some of the town's finer houses: No. 5, the **Galeria Portimão**, for stylish modern art; Nos. 8–10 for antique coins and stamps; No. 26, **Charles Jourdan**, for classic shoes at lower prices than Paris or London; No. 32, **Vinda Boutique**, for handcrafted gifts.

Move east two streets to the Rua 5 de Outubro for a further choice of shops, then walk up to the dominant **parish church**, rebuilt after the 1755 earthquake, but retaining a fine portico from the original building. Make for the square southwest of the church, with the old market at the far side, and take the pedestrianized **Rua do Comércio** leading off the square. This is the main shopping street, so browse around, then make your way back towards the harbour via its extension, the Rua Vasco da Gama. Turn left at the end of the street and along to the **Largo 1 de Dezembro**, a small park with attractively tiled benches depicting the major episodes of Portuguese history.

When the smell of fresh fish on charcoal begins to whet your appetite return to the waterside near the bridge where sardines will be sizzling on grills. Take your pick of these simple café-style restaurants and order sardines, salad and a jug of wine.

Praia da Rocha

Sleep off lunch on the **Praia da Rocha,** the most famous beach of the Algarve. You used to be able to take a horse drawn cart, but now it's a case of braving the traffic or taking a taxi (or bus). Be warned though: Praia da Rocha takes the biscuit for crass coastal development. The first resort in the Algarve (with half a dozen hotels and a handful of villas in the 1960s), it is now one long row of Costa-style development. The saving grace is the beach: a superb swath of golden sands, studded with weird rock formations and backed by cliffs sufficiently high to make the cliff top development (once you are on the beach) pale into insignificance. Sunbathe, swim or walk the length of the beach, spotting the sculptural forms along the sands: the tunnels and arches, the rocks likened to bears or humans and many other forms if you use your imagination.

By late afternoon, leave the beach for a drink in the old Fortaleza de Santa Catarina at the far eastern end of the resort. Bird's eye views across the estuary and down to the long jetty

The fort at
Ferragudo

where hopeful anglers cast their lines compensate for an uninspiring café/bar. Your evening port of call is **Ferragudo**, which you see across the estuary. It's no distance as the crow flies but you have no alternative but to get there via Portimão. Go back into town, cross the main bridge and take the second road on the right. You soon see the picturesque sight of Ferragudo's houses jostling on the hill, with beached boats on the estuary and lobster pots stacked on the quayside. Stroll around the steep cobbled streets of the centre where cats doze and locals sit in doorways fanning braziers and looking curiously at passers-by. Wander up to the fort for good views over the estuary.

Dine at the **A Lanterna Restaurant** (Tel: 082-23948, closed Sundays), on your right as you join the EN125 coming out of Ferragudo. The fish soup is excellent; so is the lamb marinaded in rosemary, garlic and mint and the duckling roasted with orange sauce. Pass by the ubiquitous *gelado* or almond tart and end the meal with a special Portuguese cake called *Pão de Ló*.

the hill, with beached boats on the estuary and lobster pots stacked on the quayside. Stroll around the steep cobbled streets of the centre where cats doze and locals sit in doorways fanning braziers and looking curiously at passers-by. Wander up to the fort for good views over the estuary.

Dine at the **A Lanterna Restaurant** (Tel: 082-23948, closed Sundays), on your right as you join the EN125 coming out of Ferragudo. The fish soup is excellent; so is the lamb marinaded in rosemary, garlic and mint and the duckling roasted with orange sauce. Pass by the ubiquitous *gelado* or almond tart and end the meal with a special Portuguese cake called *Pão de Ló*.

5. A Good Catch – Fishing Off Portimão

A day's deep sea fishing off a luxury cruiser if necessary. Reserve your rod and order your lunch in advance. (Tel: 082-85386/85483).

According to the locals the waters of the Algarve are the last unspoiled big game fishing area left in Europe. Join a deep sea cruise and the likelihood is you will catch a shark or two. Bass, conger and rays are plentiful as are the bottom-dwelling species which you can catch with hand lines while waiting for the big ones to bite. No experience is necessary (professional crew are always at hand to help) but it helps to be a good sailor. Waters are reasonably calm from June to September, but at other times be prepared for rougher seas.

For speed, comfort and the latest in gear, try the Altea or the Agualte cruisers, both of which operate from Portimão. A full day's fishing currently costs 9,600$. Non-participants, who sit and watch on the sundeck, pay 6,000$. Get details from the **harbour at Portimão** (look out for Lodewijk, the blue eyed Dutchman who runs the show) or from the **Deep Sea Fishing Centre** in town.

Boats are fully equipped with fighting chairs, outriggers, big game rods and

Monchique shepherd

reels; and the latest sonar system enables detection of fish up to a distance of 48 miles (75 km). It takes about two hours to get to the high reefs where the sharks hunt—usually about 12 miles (20 km) from the shore.

Other species likely to be lurking around are the blue shark (slim, deep blue and potentially dangerous), the copper shark and the streamlined mako, which fights like a marlin and is prized for its speed and dramatic leaps out of the sea. The tastiest of the local sharks, it frequently finds itself served up in local restaurants, masquerading as swordfish.

The biggest of the game are played from the fighting chair and can take anything up to two hours to land. Lodewijk's largest landing was a blue shark of 110 kilos (242lbs 8oz).

Those dependent on the day's fish for their dinner are in for a disappointment. All the catch goes to the crew!

6. Peaks of Monchique

Breakfast in the ancient capital of Silves; spa waters, firewater and midday meal at Caldas de Monchique; cobbled streets and convent ruins in market town of Monchique; panorama from the highest peak in the Algarve

Start your day in **Silves**, Moorish capital of the Algarve. As you approach the town, the red sandstone walls and turrets of the

Caldas de Monchique

mighty fortress make a splendid sight. The shell alone provides eloquent evidence that Silves was once far more than a sleepy rural town. Using Itinerary 8 as a guide, breakfast at the **Café Inglês** and see the castle and cathedral. By mid morning, take the EN124 west, through vines and citrus groves, stopping for sweet juicy oranges from road side vendors. When you arrive at the tiny village of Porto de Lagos (11km), take the right turning marked to Monchique. Climb up through the foothills of the Serra de Monchique, densely wooded and famed for luxuriant flora.

Your first stop is **Caldas de Monchique**, a centuries-old spa lying in a lush wooded ravine. Take the second turning on the left, marked with a yellow fountain sign (the first takes you to the bottling plant and thermal hospital), park the car and wander around this faded but still charming spa. People have been coming here since Roman times to take the spring waters of Monchique. The waters, which are meant to do wonders for rheumatism and indigestion, are warm, foul-smelling and spew from a plastic pipe.

A few drops are said to add years to your life, so give them a try or fill a flagon. Then return to the square for something which is more likely to stimulate the taste buds: the locally produced **Medronho.** This fiery distilled spirit is made from the berry of the *arbutus unedo* tree, which grows in profusion around Monchique (you can recognise it by the clusters of white or pink flowers and fleshy strawberry-like berries) and locals say you can only get the real brew in Monchique itself. It is powerful stuff and even a small glass can have an im-

Monchique, tiled bar sign

mediate effect on an empty stomach. Try
it either at the *bodega* or in the handicrafts
centre, which looks a bit like a Moorish
palace and used to be a casino. Buy a
bottle or two, then lunch on mountain
ham and chicken piri-piri in the **Restaurante Central** (Tel: 082-92203), a pleasantly old-fashioned place reminiscent of
Monchique in its heyday. The alternative is a picnic on one of the
stone benches beside the cool, babbling brook which tumbles down
the hillside at the far side of the square.

After lunch leave the Caldas (the exit is via the bottling plant
and thermal hospital), turn left and climb up amid forests of eucalyptus, cork, carob and cultivated terraces. When you get to the
market town of **Monchique**, follow the signs to the centre and
park in the large dusty Largo 5 de Outubro. Take the steep
cobbled Rua do Porto Fundo leading up to the centre. Take the
first left up a wide stairway, past the Barlefante (which serves good
tapas in a cool setting if you still happen to be hungry). Turn left
further up at the junction where you see a bar advertising 'good
port wine', along the rough cobbles and past flaking façades, into
the Largo de S. Gonçalo de Lagos, then follow the road up into
the Caminho do Convento. A short way along, turn left up a
pretty wooded track leading to the **convent**, which perches above
Monchique among weeds and camellias. To gain access walk
through the rickety old gate to the right of the building, watch
out for falling scaffolding and walk through to the main chapel.
Find the steps up to the bell tower for lovely views of Monchique
and a wide sweep of the Serra and coastline. If it is cool and you
have the stamina, there is a fine walk from here to the summit of
Fóia; you should allow about two hours for the walk to the top
and back.

Back on the Caminho do Convento, turn left and zigzag
down to the centre, detouring if you wish
to explore some of the picturesque side alleys. At the main Rua do Dr Samor Gill
turn right past white balconied houses, a
picturesque café and a tiny church
with hand painted tiles and a
carved gilt wooded gallery. Turn
left into the Rua da Igreja, passing
the Central Restaurant whose walls
are festooned with euphoric messages
from passers-by who have stopped for
a drink and stayed for four hours (do
the same if you wish), then on to the
sparkling white **parish church** at the
end of the street with its striking
Manueline doorway. Look inside the
beautifully kept interior with its

7. Monchique and Aljezur

Morning in the hills of Monchique; mountain drive to Aljezur; evening dip on the west coast.

An excursion into the hills of Monchique could easily occupy a whole day (see Itinerary 6). This rather more ambitious route, dependent on an earlier start, enables you to see Monchique before the morning charabanc of tourists arrives, and to take in the stunning and seldom used route through the mountains west of Monchique to Aljezur and the beaches beyond. Take a sweater for the cool peaks of Monchique. Try to make it to the Caldas de Monchique for breakfast no later than 9.30am.

If you are coming from Portimão, follow signs from the town side of the bridge which guide you onto the EN124. The drive takes under half an hour (not allowing for current traffic jams and diversions within Portimão) and the route is direct apart from a left turn (well marked) at Porto de Lagos, taking you onto the EN266. The terrain changes fairly rapidly, from the parched lands around the coast to the lush foothills of the Serra de Monchique, where luxuriant gardens flourish.

Your first stop is **Caldas de Monchique**, nestling in a verdant ravine and clearly signed to the left off the main road. Breakfast on fresh bread and locally produced honey at the Albergaria Velha in the square. Browse around the spa, walk up by the babbling stream, take the waters and (if it is not too early in the morning) try a nip of Monchique-made **Medronho.**

By mid morning, leave the Caldas for the market town of **Monchique**, about 7km to the north. On the way you will pass several restaurants specialising in chicken piri-piri. Refer again to Itinerary 6 to explore the cobbled streets of the town, the route to the convent and the trip up to the highest peak in Monchique at Fóia.

By the time you come down the mountain you may well be ready for a midday meal. Take your pick of either **Paraiso da Montanha** (closed Thursday) for mountain ham or chicken piri-piri; or the **Estalagem Abrigo da Montanha** for *cataplana* on the panoramic terrace. It is tempting at either location to while away the afternoon, sipping chilled wine and admiring the views. Do so if you wish but if you are to take in the Atlantic coast today, start off for Aljezur by mid afternoon.

Where the Fóia road meets

Roadside fruitstall

Carrapateira

the main road, turn right towards Portimão, then shortly right again on the road marked to Marmelete (EN267). Prepare for a rough but scenic road twisting its way through steep, partially terraced hillsides, with citrus fruit and cork trees. As you proceed, look through the road side eucalyptus trees for good views of hills beyond. In the sleepy hill village of Marmelete, follow the sign to Aljezur (17km). The road is still marked on maps as a dirt track, which deters all but the most intrepid of travellers. In fact, it is now one of the best roads in the Algarve, with exceptionally little traffic. Cut through red and ochre rocks, barren terrain and wide-open spaces, and then descend towards the coast. This is the best bit, with stunning views down to the coast and rolling, green hills between you and the sea. There is currently a brief, bumpy diversion just before Aljezur, otherwise it's fast going all the way.

The remains of a 10th century Moorish castle crowning a low hill herald the town of **Aljezur**. Drive through the dull 'new' town (built in the late 18th century as an alternative to the mosquito-infested older quarter), park just before the bridge, in the square with the tourist office and marketplace. It is possible to drive up to the **Castelo** but the going is steep and the road at the top won't taking anything much wider than a small Fiat. So leave the car, walk across the bridge, turn right through the somewhat dilapidated old Moorish village, and follow signs for the *Castelo*, up the hill and past the church. Like most castles in the Algarve it was built by the Arabs and destroyed in a series of sieges and earthquakes. Not much remains but at least there are good views all round. The track descending on the other side brings you to a peaceful local scene of whitewashed cottages with women clad in black sitting in doorways, washing flapping in the wind and cats and dogs snoozing in the sun.

From Aljezur you can either head back south (drive over the bridge, turn left for the main EN120 to Lagos) or go to the coast for a taste of the real Atlantic. Try either Arrifana, 10km southwest of Aljezur (take the turning to the right 1km south of the town), or one of the spectacular beaches west of Carrapateira. Whichever you choose, watch out for Atlantic rollers and strong currents. With time to spare stay around to watch the sun sink from the west coast of Cape St Vincent. The café at **Praia do Castelejo** just above the beach is a lovely spot for an early evening meal.

8. Silves – Ancient Capital

Breakfast and sightseeing in Silves, Moorish capital of the Algarve; afternoon on the quiet waters of the Barragem do Arade; sundowner at Algar Seco.

Poets praised its beauty and compared it to Baghdad. Historians described it as more rich and sumptuous than Lisbon. Large vessels made their way up the Arade River from Portimão, loading up with lemons, oranges and cork. Today the citrus trees still flourish (the oranges are said to be the sweetest and juiciest in the Algarve), but **Silves** is a mere shadow of its former self and the river port has long been silted up. What was not destroyed by sieges (most notably the brutal attack by Sancho I and northern crusaders in 1189) fell in the earthquake of 1755. The saving grace is the Moorish fortress, whose battlements still dominate the valley of the River Arade. The massive sandstone walls and turrets crowning the town are a fine sight as you approach from the south or east.

Park if you can on the Praça do Municipio, the square in the centre of town, and take the steep cobbled Rua da Sé up towards the castle. On your right and behind the cathedral you will find

Silves Cathedral

the **Café Inglês,** a large 1920s house attractively converted into a café/restaurant and English run (Sue is a mine of local information). Stop here for freshly brewed coffee, hot bread made in the hills and homemade marmalade.

Start your sightseeing at the **Cathedral**. Like the rest of Silves this structure has suffered the ravages of time but thanks to restoration the impression—at least that of the lofty aisles and naves—is one of pure Gothic. Some of the tombs here are said to be those of crusaders who fell in the final capture of the town. A little way further up you will see the arched gateway of the **Castelo** (open at 9am, free entrance). Within the walls gardens run riot, black cats doze and gipsy-like figures accost you with linen and lace. Nearby stands the larger-than-life statue of Sancho I, 'King of Portugal, Silves and the Algarvians', who laid seige

Silves Castle

to the Arabs' lavish stronghold. Climb up to the parapets and walk round for fine views of the valley of the River Arade and rolling hills with regimented rows of orange and lemon trees. Directly below you are the huge old cisterns and silos where the Moors took refuge before being rooted out and robbed of all their spoils by the crusaders.

Coming back down the Rua da Sé, take the Travessa do Gato to the right, a quiet alley where roosters scratch at the cobbles, canaries pipe and local women gut and wash fish for lunch. Turn left down the steps to the main square where their husbands sit on shady benches and watch the world go by. Turn right into the Rua 25 de Abril. Nip into the tourist office for an English leaflet, detailing some of the other sights of Silves (including a nearby Arab well on a site which is currently being turned into a controversial museum), then wander at leisure through the streets of the town, picking up a picnic as you go. The market (marked on the tourist office leaflet) lies on the southern side of the town, directly south of the Praca do Municipio. (The alternative to a picnic is the excellent **Restaurante Rui** in Rua Commendador Vilarinho, not far from the tourist office. Be prepared to queue, for people come for miles for the huge choice of seafood. Closed Tuesday.)

By late morning set off for the **Barragem do Arade**, a peaceful reservoir 10kms northeast of Silves. Join the main EN124 running northeast from the town (signed to São Bartolomeu de Messines) stopping as you come out of town at the 16th-century carved stone cross, the **Cruz de Portugal**, in a little pavilion on your left, and look back for the finest views of the fortress. Continue on the

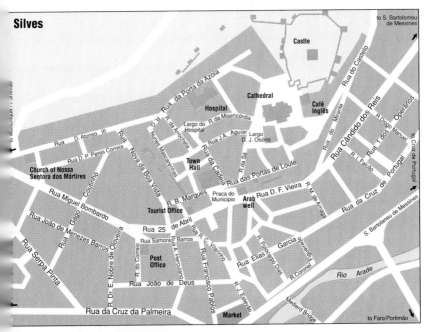

main road until you see a turning left to the *barragem*. Follow the road to a junction, just past a small restaurant, and turn left down a dirt track where figs, oranges and honey are sold by the road side and carry on until you come to a restaurant overlooking the reservoir. Rent a motor boat to explore the peaceful waters of the reservoir or take a trip across to the island for swimming, sunbathing or water sports. Even in high season this is a peaceful place, with lovely walks and plenty of good picnic spots.

Linger as long as you wish at the reservoir, then head south to Lagoa via Silves. You can browse around the **potteries of Porches** to the east (see Shopping section). Porches Pottery (on the right-hand side of the main EN125) stays open until 7pm in summer, 6pm in winter. Alternatively, go directly south from Lagoa to Carvoeiro, turn left when you get to the centre of the resort and follow the signs for **Algar Seco**. Take the flight of steps down to this beauty spot of grottoes, arches and pitted ochre rock. The waters, deep blue and transparent, are a popular haunt of snorkellers. Take a dip if you wish, then end the day with a sundowner at the taverna on the rocks. Dine at **O Lotus** (Tel: 082-52098) in Lagoa where local gourmets gather for lobster and exceptionally good *cataplana* and seafood rice.

9. Albufeira

Braving a day in the Algarve's biggest package resort.

It's the old saga of the Spanish Costas: a quaint fishing village transformed into a giant cosmopolitan resort. Hardly a paradise

for the independent traveller; yet sitting as it does in the middle of the Algarve's coast and providing probably more facilities and hotels than all the resorts to the west of it put together, it is hard to ignore. If you do brave a day here, turn a blind eye to the sprawling sky-rise outskirts and make for the

Albufeira: Fisherman's Beach

winding old alleys and vestigial traces of the fishing village. You may well find that, despite the loud bars and fish and chip shops, it is far prettier than its image might suggest.

Your starting point is the **Largo Cais Herculano**, the old fishermen's quarter behind the **Praia dos Barcos**, or Fishermen's Beach. Lobster pots, piles of nets and painted fishing smacks are all eloquent evidence that, despite the tourist invasion, the fishing industry still survives. If you can stir yourself as early as 7–7.30am you can watch the fishermen unload their catch at the wholesale fish market, and the auction nearby at the old fish market. Alternatively, arrive no later than 9–9.30am, before the tourists (who have probably been painting the town red till the early hours of the morning) start to stir. Take continental breakfast at the **Café**

Albufeira, the old town

Oceano, one of the older fishermen's haunts, which opens early in the morning. Walk inland along the Rua Candido dos Reis, which was the site of the old fruit market. This takes you northwest up to the **Largo Eng Duarte Pacheco**, the main plaza, which has been subject to ruthless modern development. Originally one of the prettier spots in town and focal point for the open air market (which used to fill the streets of the centre) its chief lure these days is a a half-litre of lager at an open air café.

Walk across the square and west into **Rua 5 de Outubro**, the main pedestrianized shopping street of town with its several pavement cafés. Browse around for shoes, ceramics and leisure wear, then come down south towards the sea, past the tourist office and through the tunnel under the Sol y Mar Hotel to see the main **Albufeira beach**. Take a swim here if the water looks inviting and there is room to manoeuvre on the beach, then retrace your steps back along the Rua 5 de Outubro. About a third of the way along the street, take a left turn into the Rua da Igreja Nova, past the parish church with its belfry and squashed onion domes. At the end of the road cross over the Praça Miguel Bombarda to the domed **Church of São Sebastião** and note the swirling finely carved motifs of the Manueline portal. Turn right and walk along the Rua Latino Coelho for splendid views of the bay. Retrace your steps to the Praça Miguel

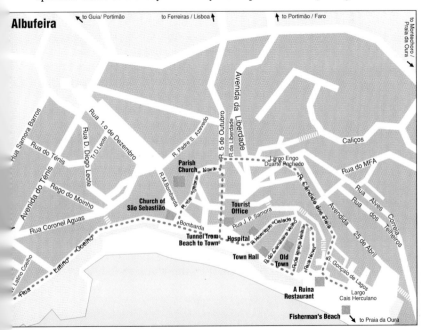

Above and *Below*: Albufeira beaches

Bombarda and note the Beach Basket restaurant with sea view terrace—a nice spot for a light lunch later—then go east into the Rua Bernardino de Sousa.

Weave your way through the narrow **alleys of the old town** by turning left into the Rua Henrique Calado. Pass the Chapel of the Misericórdia on your left, a restored 16th century church possibly built on the site of a Moorish mosque. At the end of the street turn right into the cobbled Rua do Cemeterio Velho and down to the walled promenade for good views round the bay. Follow the promenade a short way east, then turn left up the peaceful Rua da Igreja Velha, take a right at the top and go down the cobbled Rua Nova. Note at the end of the street **Mor's Country Kitchen** (advertising 'English Bif, 25 miles sea view and best looking staff'), and the Restaurant/Bar **A Ruina** perched on the cliff with roof top bar and several levels where, when it's time for lunch, you can eat fish fresh from the market and look down on the bay. Prices here are on the steep side and service in high season is brusque, but for location you can't beat it.

Alternatively, return to the Beach Basket or try one of the

cheaper tavernas in town serving a simple plate of sardines, salad and a jug of wine.

If your afternoon priority is a beach, you can try either the **Olhos de Agua** to the east of Albufeira, or **São Rafael** to the west, both less crowded than Albufeira, but by no means undiscovered. Unfortunately, you can't hire a fishing boat (and fisherman) from Albufeira as you can in some other resorts, but there is a small converted trawler which takes a few tourists to deserted beaches and grottoes along this lovely stretch of coast. (Telephone in advance: 089-

10. Hill Village Tour from Albufeira

Morning in hill villages of Alte and Salir; lunch at Querença; afternoon shopping/sightseeing in Loulé.

Alte is arguably the prettiest of all the hill villages, more by virtue of well-kept, whitewashed houses, clean cobbled streets and lush gardens than architectural merit. The area is delightful for walks and picnics in the hills. Avoid Saturday afternoons in season when a charabanc of tourists may well descend on the village. If you are lucky your visit may coincide with the monthly market.

If you are coming from Albufeira, you could make a brief diversion to the village of **Paderne** for its Manueline church and castle ruins; and/or to **São Bartolomeu** de Messines, 12km to the northwest of it, to see another example of the Manueline in the curious red sandstone church with its twisted stone columns.

At Alte, park at the Fonte Pequena (Little Fountain Inn) beside the mountain stream and walk to the centre, passing on the way pristine patios, balconies brimming with plants and brilliant splashes of colour from hibiscus, oleander and geraniums. Look inside the church, filled with flowers, and embellished with blue and white glazed tiles and colourful religious statuary.

If it is shut get the key from the lady who lives in the first house (red door) of Rua Dr Manuel Figueiredo. Take the steps to your left as you face the church door, and the street is

The village of Alte

the first one on the left. Stop for a drink in one of the cafés lying in the shadow of the church. If there are locals around they tend to patronise the **Altense** just below the entrance and where, morning dews or showers permitting, you can join them for a saucer of snails and Sagres lager. At the other end of the village, on your way back to the Fonte Pequena, take a glimpse at the Baroque chapel on the small square and the adjoining museum with its idiosyncratic collection of metal pots, rat traps, cow bells and 1930s photos of the Alte Band.

On a scorching day cool off at the **Fonte Grande** (beyond Fonte Pequena) where there is a waterfall of sorts and stone benches in the shade of trees. Alte is famed for the purity of its springs and people used to come for miles to collect the waters.

Take the main EN124 going east out of the village and drive for about 12kms through unspoilt rural scenery

until you come to **Salir** on your right. Another 'hill village', this one is not so orderly as Alte, but has the distinct advantage of being off the tourist itineraries. Follow the signs to the *Castelo* which, as you will see, is now no more than chunks of old Arab fortress walls integrated with village houses. Park the car near the tiny bar and wander round this simple little oasis where patios overflow with plants, geraniums tumble over stone walls and dogs nap peacefully in the sunshine.

From here you can look across to the centre of Salir where the church dominates and the houses are jumbled on the hillside below. Have a look round, then return to the road you came in on and follow it southward (towards Loulé) through the hills and past villages too tiny to be marked on maps.

At Ponte de Tor (7km) turn left for **Querença** and continue for about 4km until you see a small road to the right marked to the village. You come into the village square where the pretty Baroque church is set against a background of green hills. Take the road at the far side of the square, then proceed a little further: on your left, you will see the entrance to the **Quinta do Olival** restaurant (Tel: 089-62969). Stop here for lunch, preferably on the panoramic terrace surveying a huge sweep of hills to the south. Try

Qurença main square

some of the local specialities and end with almond cake. (Twelve-year-old Veronica, who has been studying English at the local school, will help with any language problems.)

Your afternoon destination is **Loulé**. Turn left out of the restaurant, and follow the signposts for Loulé, taking the main EN396 south through hilly terrain forested with pine, eucalyptus and cork. At Loulé, turn left at the major crossroads, then left again at the roundabout, and park your car on the main tree lined boulevard. See Itinerary 11 and spend your afternoon in the town shopping for local handicrafts and souvenirs, sightseeing or just wandering at your leisure.

11. Lunch in Loulé

**Market town of Loulé: sights, shops
and market stalls. To see Loulé at its
liveliest go on a Saturday morning when
the main market is in full swing.**

If your starting point is Faro, make a
brief diversion to take in the **Igreja de
São Lourenço**, a gem of a church set on
a hillock above the EN125, east of Almansil. To get there go about 2.5km beyond the turn-off to Loulé, take the narrow turning to the right marked to São
Lourenço and you will come up to the
church. Contrast the frenzy of the EN125
with this quiet oasis, where cool blue
and white tiles embellish every inch of
walls and vaulting, setting off the sumptuous gilded altar. Leave the church (and
a few *escudos* for the upkeep), turn right
onto the EN125, right again at Almansil
and follow the signs to Loulé. When you
get to the town (7km from Almansil),
ignore the outlying modern sprawl and
head for the centre, parking if you can
on the wide tree lined boulevard, Avenida
José da Costa Mealha.

Start with the **market**, an unmistakable mock-Moorish structure
with pink onion-shaped domes. On a Saturday the surrounding
streets will be packed with stalls selling local produce: buckets of
black and green olives, baskets of beans, sacks of almonds, strings

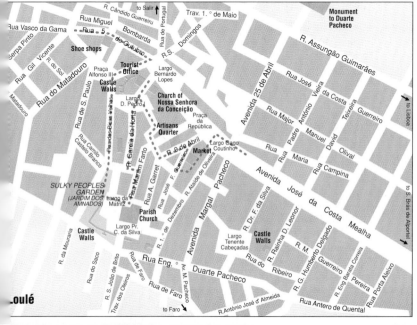

of sausages, boxes of oranges, bunches of coriander. Take your pick of the produce, then make your way inside the covered market (a daily feature) where baby chicks and ducklings are sold in shoe boxes and local black-clad peasants squat alongside the walls with a basket of eggs or a pair of rabbits huddled in a box. On the far side, stalls sell cheap chunky earthenware plates, pots and vases at excellent prices.

Leave the market on this side and turn right along the Rua José F Guerreiro, then sharp left down the cobbled **Rua 9 de Abril**. Listen for the sound of hammers and sanders and peek into the narrow doorways of workshops where local artisans are making copper and brass pots and pans. Turn right at the crossroads, past the Free Times Bar, and follow the road right down to the tourist office, passing en route the law courts and a convent converted into a stylish modern art gallery. The tourist office sits in a particularly pleasant courtyard across

the Rua D Paio Peres Correia, with the old castle walls above. Take the steps to the left of the office for good views from the castle battlements.

Coming out of the courtyard turn left and cross the road for the inconspicuous-looking **Church of Nossa Senhora da Conceição**. If it's locked get the key from the frail old lady at No. 27 opposite, encouraging her with a few *escudos*. The key opens the brown painted door to the left of the church. Walk through a tiny makeshift chapel and enter the church through the entrance on the right. The interior is a delightful combination of gilded carving and blue and white *azulejos* depicting biblical scenes. Retrace your steps, past the tourist office, then diagonally cross the Largo D. Pedro I into Rua Garcia da Horta, a cobbled alley of pretty houses; turn left at the top, then right into Rua Martim Farto. From here you'll see the lofty bell tower of the **parish church**. Walk up to the square, and into the church through the carved portal. Note inside the finely tiled panels, Manueline carving and curious capitals. If the church is closed, try to get the key from the priest who lives at 19 Calçada dos Sapateiros, the street at the right hand corner of the square if you are standing with your back to the church.

When you come out of the church take a seat under the palms in the charming gardens opposite (closed at lunch time) and try to work out why they are called the *Jardim dos Amuados,* or Sulky People's

Garden. Turn down the Calçada dos Sapateiros (see above), then down steps to the left which bring you into the Rua Martim Moniz. Turn right here and see the startling contrast of old and modern Loulé. Drop into the pottery workshop on your right at Nos. 43–45 (if open), pause at the Restaurante Bica Velha at Nos. 17–19 which claims to occupy the oldest building in town. Note the menu in case you want to return for lunch (good bets are prawns in hot sauce and grey mullet with fennel and *Medronho*). Carry on down the road until you come to the square, Praça Afonso III, and turn right into the Rua da Barbaça where there are more artisans and the shops are full of handicrafts. Turn left into the Rua 5 de Outubro, a pedestrianized street with shoe shops and open air cafés.

Lunch either at the **Bica Velha** or for something with a bit more Portuguese ambience try **O Avenida** (closed Sunday) above the Shell petrol station on the Avenida José da Costa Mealha. Here sardines, sausage, salad and olives are thrown in, so there's no need to order a starter. If it is not a Saturday (when shops close at 1pm) or Sunday, spend any spare time in the afternoon browsing around for leather goods (particularly shoes), ironwork, copper, brass and palm, cane and wickerwork.

12. Capital City

Morning in Faro, strolling around the harbour and historic city; shopping and lunch; optional trip to Praia de Faro.

Faro's international airport opened in 1965 and since then tourists have been pouring in. The majority see no more than the view from the skies: a large, concrete sprawl, separated from the ocean by long thin sand spits and a series of islets. Admittedly, Faro's architectural make-up has been severely impoverished by sieges, raids and earthquakes, but to ignore the inner city, where relics of the old walls, traces of Gothic and much of the Baroque survive, is to miss one of the finest old quarters of the Algarve.

If you visit in high season, arrive early in order to avoid parking problems and to see the main sights before the intense midday heat. Bear in mind too that the Cathedral closes at 12pm and most sites are shut at weekends.

Park close to the waterfront and start the day with a stroll around the palm-lined harbour. Stop for coffee/breakfast in the harbour side gardens which, despite placards for hamburgers, have a good deal of southern charm; or breakfast in the brasserie-styled **Café Aliança** just across the road in the Rua Dr Francisco Gomes.

The inner or historic centre lies to the south. Approach it through the **Arco da Vila**, a handsome Italianate arch flanked by two Ionian columns and topped by a belfry whose high vantage point provides a home for nesting storks. The figure in the niche above the arch is St Thomas Aquinas, who was later made patron saint of the city for saving it from the plague in the early part of the 17th century.

The cobbled, whitewashed Ruo do Municipio leads up from the archway to the **Largo da Sé**, *Largo* being the cobbled square and *Sé* the omnipresent Cathedral. Note the old Bishop's Palace to your right, the Town Hall to your immediate left and then enter the heavy Gothic portal on the west side of the Cathedral. The cool, spacious interior is a welcome respite on a hot summer's day. Gone is most of the Gothic, but there are some very fine 18th-century glazed tiles in the side chapels, notably those in the second chapel on the left and the last chapels on either side of the naves.

Coming out of the Cathedral turn left and explore the quiet primitive quarter in and around the cobbled Rua do Arco, then turn along the Rua Professor Norberto da Silva, where pots of plants hang on faded façades and the only sounds (till low flying

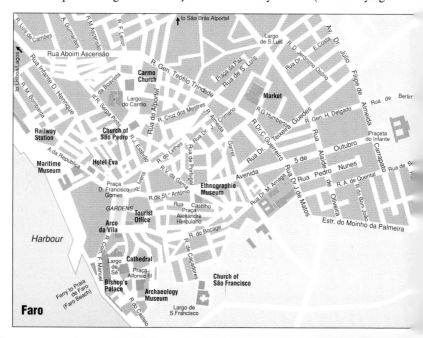

aircraft or Vespas whiz by) are canaries trilling in their cages. Pass the Taverna da Sé on your right and come into the **Praça Afonso III**, dominated by a statue of the determined looking Dom Afonso III (1210–79), who effectively put an end to Moorish hegemony in the Algarve. Find No.14 at the bottom of the square on your right for the **Archaeological Museum** (9.30am–12.30pm, 2pm–5.30 pm, Monday to Friday, entrance 50$). The exhibits, grouped according to epoch, from prehistoric to neoclassical, have an exceptionally beautiful setting in the quiet cloistered galleries of a restored Renaissance convent. The only drawback is the lack of English labelling. Upper galleries (paintings, pottery, silver and furniture) are unlikely to inspire but go up for good views of the gargoyles on the cloisters.

Before you leave the old centre note the menu at the **Cidade Velha** on the east side of the Largo da Sé, the only restaurant in the historic city, which also happens to be one of the best (and most expensive) in Faro. Typical dishes are fresh clams with garlic and coriander, succulent prawns in chilli sauce and filet of pork with dates, walnuts and port. If this whets the appetite book a table for lunch later on.

Leave the old city via the Arco de Repousa off the Praça Afonso III. The arch is best viewed from the far side. Turn right into the large desolate Largo de São Francisco and make for the church beside the barracks. (The Faro Infantry occupy the adjoining monastery.) If the church is closed, ring the bell on the door to the left of the entrance. With luck it should open automatically. Cross the pretty courtyard and enter the church by the door on the right. A modest façade belies an internal extravaganza of blue and gold, created by the sumptuous gilded and lacquered woodcarvings and the glazed tiles with scenes from the life of St Francis. Leaving the church, turn right into the Rua de Caçadores and carry on until you come to the Praça Alexandre Herculano. The Casa de Lumena (an above average pension) used to belong to one of Faro's big fishing magnates. Continue till you come to the Praça da Liberdade. On the corner to your right is a large building containing the **Ethnographic Museum** (Open 9.30am–12.30pm, 2pm–5.30pm weekdays, entrance 50$), an interesting but unremarkable collection depicting traditional Algarvian life: tuna nets, lobster pots, baskets, beehives, a

Feeding pigeons in the cathedral square

replica of a peasant house and a typical coloured fishing smack with an eye to ward off the devil.

Exiting the museum, take the left turn off the square into the pedestrianized **Rua de Santo António**. This is the main shopping street in Faro. The swirling mosaic pattern of the cobblestones, and the elegant upper storeys of the buildings are the saving grace of this otherwise modernized thoroughfare. The rest of the street has been given over to cafés and fast food outlets. Stop for a drink in an open air café, watch the world go by, then spend what remains of the morning singling out the best of the shops. (Oberon at No. 67, first shop on your right, is very tempting for leather.)

Shops shut at 1pm at which point you can either return to the Cidade Velha (see above) or choose a restaurant closer by. At the end of Rua Santo António, take a right turn up to the Praça

Ferreira de Almeida and look around here for inviting fish restaurants. One of the best is the **Recife** at No. 32 Rua Vasco do Gama (east of the square), which serves an excellent lobster *cataplana*; or in the same street the simpler **Marisqueira Vasco do Gama** where locals go for seafood and TV.

After lunch but not before 3pm, take the Rua José Estevão northwest from the Praça Ferreira de Almeida. Pass the church of São Pedro on your right and, further on, come into the Largo do Carmo, with its unmistakable twin-belfried Baroque **Church of Carmo** standing

Left: San Francisco church;
Right: Antique shop

somewhat incongruously among modern high-rise blocks. The interior is embellished with lavish woodcarvings, but far more striking and what everyone comes to see is the macabre **Capela dos Ossos** (Chapel of Bones). Ask the sacristan and you will be taken to this tiny chapel hidden in the cemetery at the back of the church. If you have visited the Church of São Francisco in Évora you will know what to expect. If not, prepare to face the chilling bones and grinning skulls of 1,254 monks and parishioners covering the walls of the chapel.

Make your way back to the harbour and pay at least a brief visit to the **Maritime Museum** in the Harbour Master's building, northwest of the harbour. Here you will find a fascinating collection of fishing paraphernalia, such as tuna harpoons, fish traps, fishing tackle, nets and cages, plus the added (and rare) bonus of good notes in English.

Wind down at the **Praia de Faro**, not one of the loveliest Algarve beaches but quite sufficient for a dip or session of wind surfing and rowing (fishing equipment provided) and pleasant to get to if you take the ferry. The terminal is at the southern end of the harbour. Boats only go in good weather. Ask at the tourist office, near the *Arco da Vila,* for times.

13. Cultural Core

Morning sightseeing/shopping in Faro; leisurely lunch, Roman ruins and Rococo Palace in Estói; village of Moncarapacho and

views from Serra de San Miguel; fish dinner in Olhão.

This is a short tour (30kms), but one which covers several high spots of the eastern half of the Algarve, both cultural and geographical. Avoid Sunday and Monday when sites are closed. (Conversely, if you happen to be anywhere near Estói on the first Sunday of the month, don't miss the 'gipsy' market.) Park as close to Faro harbour as you can and spend the morning sightseeing. Cover as many sites from Itinerary 12 as you wish, but make the **Centro Histórico** your top priority and bear in mind that the Cathedral closes at 12pm. By late morning leave behind you the hubbub and heat

57

of the city and head for the quiet countryside north of Faro. The simplest way of getting to **Estói** (pronounced Shtoe-ee) is to head west from the harbour, following signs for Faro airport and Portimão, then turn right when you see the signs for São Brás de Alportel. This will bring you onto the EN2 where the sprawling suburbs of Faro gradually give way to groves of orange and lemon trees. Carry on until you see a fork right for Estói (you are now roughly 11kms from Faro), followed by another right turn. Note the *Ruínas de Milreu* (Roman ruins) on your left before the village which you will return to later.

Lunch is a choice of two extremes. Either join the locals in the cheap **Café Retiro dos Arcos** (inconspicuously signed on the left shortly before the church) for generous helpings of charcoal grilled chicken or chops, or treat yourself to the more hedonistic pleasures of **Monte do Casal** (Tel: 089-91503), where you can indulge in smoked potted quail mousse and salmon trout by the pool or in the converted coach house. This country house restaurant is set in lovely gardens 3kms from Estói with views south to the sea. To get there follow the yellow signs from the centre of Estói. The place is not very Portuguese (English run with a chef who trained with the Savoy group), but it's an ideal spot to unwind

Moncarapacho Museum

after the frenzy of Faro. The sleepy simple village of Estói gives you no clue that it is the setting of the most lavish manor house in the Algarve, which lies behind high stone walls close to the centre. After lunch but not before 3pm, take the road to your left as you face the steps of the church, and try the gate at the end of the road. Opening times are entirely *ad hoc* and you may be unlucky. If not, walk through the gate, along an alley of palm trees. Soon you will see the terraces and gardens heralding the Rococo **Palácio of the Condes de Carvalhal**. Built in the 18th century and added to in a variety of styles, it is a charming (if not aesthetically satisfying) faded pink villa. You can't go inside (by all accounts it is decaying by the minute and some say haunted by the first cousin of the last Count of Estói), so content yourself with ambling around a fantasy garden of fountains, balustraded terraces, neoclassical statues and sweet smelling flowerbeds running wild. Note the fine tiled panels along the stone stairways, the semi-clothed statues, the

busts of notables and—hidden below the main balustrade —a replica of Canova's *Three Graces.* Faro's *Câmara* bought the palace two years ago for some trivial sum; now there are rumours that it is up for grabs again.

Return to the **ruins of Milreu** and park the car by the gates. Somewhat scant and overgrown as seen from the roadside, these Roman remains deserve a good half hour, if only for the mosaics. Of the original Roman villa, you can still see fragments of capitals, relics of kitchens and baths; but the richest spoils—statues, imperial busts, ceramics, gravestones and mosaics—were taken and distributed among museums in Portugal (Faro Archaeological and Lagos Regional Museums, among them) and private collections. To locate mosaics of fish and crustaceans consult the map in English on the site. The big solid water sanctuary, rising above the ruins on the south side, looks more like a Gallic/Roman temple and was, in fact, used as a church when the Visigoths took over the region.

Leave Estói on the Olhão road, then take the turning left to Moncarapacho (passing the Monte do Casal). After about 8km, cross the main EN398 and take the road into the centre of Moncarapacho. Park in the main square and amble around this quiet and simple Algarve village. At siesta time dogs will be dozing in the shade of the church, old men drinking in *tasca* bars and young ones glued to TV soaps in the local café. The finest piece of architecture in the village is the carved Renaissance portal of the parish church in the square. The hours of the near-

The back streets of Olhão

by chapel and adjoining museum are restricted to 11am to 3pm Monday, Wednesday and Friday, but you might try your powers of persuasion and ask the local priest who lives opposite the main church to show you round the idiosyncratic collection of archaeological finds and sacred art. The next door chapel of Santo Cristo, traditionally famed as a place of miracles, is covered with fine yellow, blue and white *azulejos*.

As evening approaches, return to the EN398, turn right and take the first left, a narrow road marked inconspicuously Serra de San Miguel. If it is cool and a five-mile hike up the hillside does not daunt you, go by foot and enjoy the scenery. The road winds up through lemon and orange groves, carobs and figs, then opens out onto red rocky slopes of macchia and wild

flowers. For centuries the mountain was seen as sacred and pilgrims came here to seek spiritual solace or rub themselves in its supposedly therapeutic earth. Today it is still a beauty spot, though somewhat spoiled by the radio station that sits at the top. Return to the main EN398 and turn right for Olhão. When you get to the town, follow the signs for the *Mercados*, past the fishing port, and park on the main Avenida 5 de Outubro close to the covered market-places. Browse around the winding alleys of the fishermen's quarter. As evening falls and the smell of fresh fish, sizzling on charcoal, starts to stimulate the appetite, return to the Avenida 5 de Outubro and dine on whatever fish takes your fancy.

14. Off the Beaten Track – São Bras to Tavira

Breakfast at São Brás de Alportel, spectacular mountain drive up to Cachopo and down to Tavira.

This 70km tour through remote hills and mountains is particularly pretty in spring when slopes are dotted with the white blossoms of rock roses. On a really hot day leave the trip until late afternoon or early evening when the sun silhouettes the hills and mountains.

For a morning tour, begin the day at the Pousada at São Brás de Alportel. Equivalent to the Spanish *paradores*, the Portuguese *pousadas* are state run, off the beaten track, usually with good views. The Pousada at São Brás is no exception, sitting on a hill and surveying a wide sweep of the eastern Algarve. To get there take the main EN2 Lisbon road north from the town of São Brás. After a couple of kilometres take the right turn marked to the Pousada, along a drive of fig trees. Breakfast, at 1,000$, is no giveaway, but by Algarvian standards it is exceptionally good and you can help yourself to as much as you like and enjoy the views at the same time.

Return to the Lisbon road and head north through eucalyptus trees and cork oaks. Just after Barranco do Velho (13km), take the road marked to Cachopo. You'll now be travelling through a very remote hilly region of the Algarve, far removed from the hubbub of the coast. Spring is the prettiest time, when the slopes are deep green and the cistus and broom are in flower, but all year long

Tavira river and fish market

covering the hillsides, the pine trees and the tall eucalyptus, often lopped off and lying by the wayside.

Stop for a drink at **Cachopo,** a simple village with a couple of bars and café-restaurants serving seafood. From here you can either take an extended scenic route, north to Alcoutim and then south along the River Guadiana, or take the EN397 to Tavira, which snakes down through a spectacular landscape of rolling hills. The journey is less than 40kms but the winding road and rough patches make it feel a lot longer. There are some lovely views if you dare take your eyes off the twisting road. You won't see much civilisation here—just the odd donkey cart laden with grass, brown and white speckled goats grazing on the hillside and the occasional white farmhouse nestling in a valley. Spare an hour or two for the elegant centre of Tavira. Refer to Itinerary 17 for the main things to see and suggestions for lunch.

15. The Sotavento Alhão and Tavira

Fish market in Olhão; lunch in Tavira; swim at Monte Gordo; castle at Castro Marim.

What the Sotavento lacks in dramatic coastal scenery—saltpans, sand bars and citrus fruits—is to a large degree compensated for by the refreshing absence of package-style holiday resorts and the fact that it has two of the most interesting places to visit along the entire Algarve coast: Olhão and Tavira. The word 'Sotavento' means leeward and the coast along here is partially protected by a shoreline of sand spits. Arrive in **Olhão** as early as you can to see the fish market in full swing (see Itinerary 16). Take plenty of film and a flash gun to snap the fishwives laying out the purchases in big flat baskets, and record the sheer variety of fish and seafood

piled up high on the stalls. Spend an hour exploring the alleys of the fishermen's quarter and view the flat roofed houses and forest of chimneys and aerials from the belfry of the parish church.

By mid morning rejoin the EN125, following the signs for Vila Real and head for Tavira (22km). The road is first-class for the Algarve but the scenery is uninspiring, with straggling development and real estate ads interspersed among the wayside carob and lemon trees. Slow down as you get to the centre of Luz de Tavira to note, on your left, the doorway of the parish church, which is a good example of Manueline architecture. Further on, look out for wayside *artesanato* stalls

Castro Marim

—a good source for *cataplanas*, liquor stills, rugs and basketry. Take the turning off to **Tavira** and, as you come towards the centre, follow the signs to Vila Real, which will bring you to the main **Praça da República**. Park here if you can. From this attractive square you are a stone's throw from the key features of the city: the old stone bridge, the riverside gardens with their stately palms, the marketplace, the castle and two main churches. Begin with a leisurely drink in one of the open air cafés facing the gardens and river. Consult Itinerary 17 for the main attractions of the town, then spend the rest of the morning sightseeing, shopping, browsing around the back streets or taking a pedalo along the river. Have lunch at one of the recommended restaurants.

From Tavira take the road to Vila Real (23km), past lush farmlands of fig, carob and citrus fruits. Side roads lead off to beaches, but save your swim until **Monte Gordo**, 3km before Vila Real. The waters are the warmest you will find along the Algarve coast, so take a dip or, if time permits, hire a wind surfer.

Leave for **Castro Marim** at the latest by 4pm. If you want to go in style ask at the tourist office (east of the casino on the beach) if the horse drawn carriages are running. By car you return to the EN125, turn right, follow the road for nearly 3km and take the left turn marked Beja, Lisbon and Castro Marim. Drive through the region's nature reserve, slow down to spot waders in the lagoons, then head towards the mighty ruins of the 13th-century fortress of **Castro Marim.** Walk up and do a full circuit of the battlements for a 360-degree panorama and bird's eye view of Spain. Head back from here or end the day with a drink at one of the cafés in the stately square of **Vila Real de Santo António**.

PLUNGING POODLES

It loves to swim and dive and has membranes on its paws. It plunges deep, guides fish into nets and can catch them between its teeth.

The curly-haired Algarve 'poodle' has been assisting the fishermen of the Algarve for centuries. It formed part of the crew of caravels and galleons and is known to have saved sailors and fishermen from drowning in the high seas.

With the changes in fishing traditions in the 1950s and 1960s this extraordinary breed was in real danger of extinction. But there are still about 1,000 thoroughbreds in the country. And half a dozen of them are kept in captivity in the Ria Formosa Nature Reserve near Olhão. They are very congenial creatures, more like large curly-haired mongrels than poodles. If you want to have a look, ask for directions from the tourist office in Olhão (Rua do Comércio), then ask at the nature reserve for permission to look at them.

16. Port of Olhão

A day in and around the port of Olhão; fish and food markets; the fishermen's quarters, fish lunch; ferry to the islands.

In 1808, 17 intrepid fishermen took a small boat all the way to Rio de Janeiro to tell the exiled Portuguese King, João vi, that Napoleon's troops had left his kingdom. As a reward, the village on the sands was raised to the status of a town and titled Olhão da Restauração. The fishing industry expanded, canneries were created and, by the mid 19th century, Olhão was a prosperous port. Fish markets, fishermen's quarters and nudist beaches are not everyone's cup of tea, and the average Algarve tourist has probably never heard of Olhão. But for the independent traveller, this has to be the most underrated place in the Algarve.

Make an early start to see the pick of the morning catch before it is whisked off by the local restaurateurs. (The lobsters will have gone already.) When you reach the town, follow the signs for *Porto de Pesca/Mercados,* which take you the broad Avenida 5 de Outubro. Stop at the ferry landing terminal to enquire about the departure times of boats going to the islands in the afternoon. Then stroll through the well-nurtured **Patrão Joaquim Lopes gardens,** beside palms, flowerbeds and a carp pond with ducks and terrapins. Make for the covered **markets** beyond, two distinctive redbrick turreted buildings, one for fruit and vegetables, the other devoted to fish and seafood.

Start with the fish market (the far building) and spend as long as you like looking at the amazing variety of seafood: sea bass and sea bream, crab claws and crayfish, whole conger eel, huge chunks of tuna, heaps of gleaming sardines, writhing inky squid, starfish and spider crabs, live cockles twitching in trays of water. Exit the market on the waterfront side where coloured smacks are moored and fish hang drying like coat hangers.

Nip into the neighbouring food market for oranges,

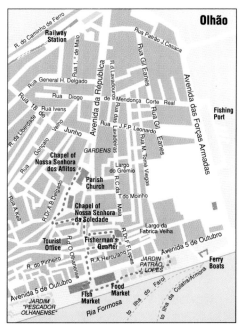

Donkey cart

dates or apricots; then stroll around the **fishermen's quarter**. Traditionally likened to an African Kasbah, it is still very picturesque, with narrow winding alleys, cubistic houses, flaking white façades, chimneys and and the occasional belvedere where the wives of fishermen looked out to sea. Surprisingly, this is no legacy of Moorish occupation, Olhão was founded in the 18th century and the Moorish style developed only through commercial links with North Africa.

Start at the palm lined open square opposite the area between the two markets. The most characteristic streets are just further up from here on the right. Start with the roughly cobbled Rua J dos Santos and wriggle your way up to the Rua Santo Estevão. Note the flat Moorish architecture, tiled façades, 'claw' door knockers and washing hanging on street corners. In the Rua Santo Estevão, at No. 31, beside his cobbler's shop, **Marío Caleça** may be playing *fado* on his Portuguese guitar. Pause at the doorway and, recognising you as foreign (photos of fans abroad line his shelves), he may suggest some Frank Sinatra—or more *fado* if you prefer. Turn right at the end of the street, then take your first left into the Rua do Comércio, a pedestrian shopping street with attractive patterned paving and façades above modern shop fronts. Admire them before they come under the demolition order. Some are already being torn down to give way to drab modern styles. Turn left down the Rua da Soledade into a small square overlooked by a white Baroque chapel. Turn right to get to the main

Drying fish in Olhão

Olhão rooftops

parish church. Go inside and ask at the sacristy (top left-hand corner) for access to the belfry. Climb to the top for good shots of the flat topped roofs, chimneys, terraces and TV aerials of the old quarter. Try to avoid a visit on the hour or the vibrations of the bell may shatter your eardrums.

Exit the church and go to the rear of the building (facing the Avenida da República). Here you will see women praying at a little chapel where candles burn among wax *ex votos* of human legs, arms and faces. This is the **Chapel of Nossa Senhora dos Aflitos**. Here fishermen's wives have traditionally come to pray for their men when there are storms at sea.

Return to the Avenida 5 de Outubro and choose one of the fish restaurants for lunch. You are unlikely to be disappointed whether you opt for live lobsters, swordfish, bream or bass (**Kinkas** opposite the fruit and vegetable market is good) or a simple plate of sardines. For the latter try **O Boté**, beyond the fish market on the right, and one of several café-like haunts of the locals where you can tuck into as many grilled sardines as you like, with salad, for 500$, then wash it down with tumblers full of *vinho da casa*.

After lunch explore the tiny streets of the fishermen's quarter behind, even more African-looking and fascinating than the quarter described above. Watch the fishermen sitting on makeshift stools in the street, mending lobster pots and knotting hooks to long lines. Women will probably be slicing or washing fish, or fanning a few sardines grilling on hot coals. To get into the heart of this ethnic quarter take the Rua de Barreta off the Avenida 5 de Outubro (almost opposite the bandstand in the gardens) and work your way east.

Spend the rest of the day on one of Olhão's pair of offshore islands. Both are serviced by ferries and feature sandy beaches but, for preference, opt for the **Ilha da Armona**. The trip across to this long, skinny sand spit takes 15 minutes. When you get to the island, walk for about a kilometre to the far side in order to reach the unspoilt beaches and sand dunes. Strip off (literally if you like) and spend the afternoon swimming and soaking up the sun.

17. Morning Tour of Tavira

Sightseeing and browsing in the town of Tavira; Cataplana lunch; optional foray into the interior or afternoon on the beach

Straddling the broad River Gilão and filled with fine old houses and over 30 churches, **Tavira** retains an elegance that most towns in the Algarve have lost. Holiday makers based west of Faro rarely bother to pay it a visit and the town and surroundings remain relatively uncommercialized. Expect gradual changes however with the completion of the international bridge across the River Guadiana (1992) and a motorway link with Spain.

Arrive no later than 10am to secure a parking space in the main square, **Praça da República**. From here wander through the riverside **gardens** where stately palms sway gently in the breeze, and admire the view from the riverside. Look upstream to the stone arched bridge whose foundations go back to Roman times. Walk to the far end of the gardens, through the green wrought iron gates of the market and take your pick of figs, almonds and other fruits from the Sotavento's lush farmlands. The morning's catch will be displayed at the far end of the market. Tavira was not so long ago a major port for tuna fishing and a little further along the river the upturned hulks of old boats are reminders of the bloody battles between the tuna and the fishermen, aptly described as the 'bullfights of the sea'. Return to the Praça da República (stopping if you wish at one of the pleasant open air cafés by the gardens for coffee or late breakfast), locate the tourist office under the reconstructed medieval arches of the town hall and take the cobbled steps opposite which lead up the castle. On your way up note the finely carved Renaissance portal of the **Church of Misericórdia** (if it is open, which normally it is not, go inside to see the gilded woodwork and *azulejos*); turn left up towards the **Church of Santa Maria do Castelo**, built on the site of a former mosque. If closed, try the door of the sacristan at No. 50 Calçada de D Ana (the road to the right and parallel as you look at the belfry), and enjoy a brief, friendly guided tour in Portuguese of this re-

Previous pages: Selling the sardine catch;
Above and *Right*: Tavira

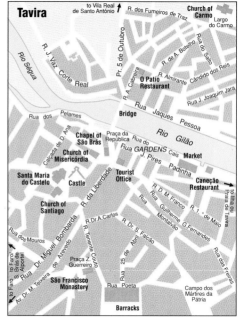

freshingly simple, white-washed church. The chancel houses the tomb of of Dom Paio Peres Correia, who liberated large chunks of the Algarve from the Moors, and an inscription commemorating the seven Christian knights who, during a truce, were killed by Moors while out hunting near Tavira. Leave the church and visit the neighbouring gardens within the castle walls (shut mornings at weekends and holidays off season) for good views of roof tops and domes.

Make your way back to the central square, cross over the bridge, noting the plaque on this side commemorating the bravery of the locals when they repelled the invading troops of King Juan I of Castile in 1383–5. On the left bank of the river look back at the skyline of church spires, tiled roofs and castle ramparts. Wander at leisure on this side of the river, starting with the Rua Dr António Cabreira to peek into artisans' workshops and an intriguing antique/bric-a-brac shop on the left as you go down. On the opposite side of the road take a look at the menu in the O Pátio restaurant, a possibility for lunch later on (see below). Spend what remains of the morning nosing around the back streets, *tasca* bars and boutiques of the west bank. For lunch try one of the local *cataplanas*—a soup-*cum*-casserole served in a special domed tin or copper vessel. Supplies of fish permitting, you have the choice of lobster *cataplana* at **O Pátio**, clams *cataplana* at the **Imperial**, facing the public gardens (not as grand as it sounds) or the slightly cheaper **O Canecão** further along the same road, past the market, which also serves clams with rabbit (in season) and excellent fish soup and seafood rice. You could be brave and ask for a glass or two of the heady Tavira wine. With spare time in the afternoon, you may choose to follow Itinerary 14, looping up to Cachopo through lovely hill scenery or, if it is too hot for touring, join the sun seekers on the **Ilha da Tavira**, a sand spit lying offshore and reached by ferry from Tavira beach. The terminal is about 2kms from the centre of town, past the marketplace and through the saltpans.

18. Borderlines

Half-day visit to the border towns of Vila Real de Santo António and Ayamonte in Spain.

For a real taste of Spain you need to go as far as Seville. **Ayamonte**, an ordinary border town, can't compare with the famous cities of Andalusia, but the ferry trip is quite fun and very cheap. Remember your passport, but there's no need for Spanish pesetas. Escudos, pounds, dollars—anything seems to go. A bridge spanning the River Guadiana and linking Spain with Portugal will be complete by 1992, but the ferry service will carry on operating.

Allow half an hour or more for **Vila Real de Santo António**, a town submerged in the sea in the 17th century, then rebuilt in 1774 in a matter of months. The mastermind behind the speedy reconstruction was the Marquês de Pombal, Chief Minister to King José I, who had already raised parts of Lisbon from their ruins after the disastrous 1755 earthquake. For Vila Real he adopted the same grid pattern, paving and uniform façades as he used in the *Baixa* quarter. All the materials, even the hewn stone and prefabricated window and door frames, were carted from the capital—the irony being that, a short while later, stone quarries were discovered in the vicinity of Vila Real. Make for the main *Praça do Marquês de Pombal*, a handsome square with black and white mosaic paving radiating from a central obelisk.

Sit under one of the sweet smelling orange trees lining the square or order a drink in one of the open air cafés.

Head two blocks east, cross the main Avenida da República into well-watered gardens. See ferries plying across the water, waders nosing in the mud and the whitewashed houses of Ayamonte on the Spanish side of the river. Go north up the Avenida, past some dignified residences on your left with Macau roofs (pitched and curved in Oriental fashion), and make for the tourist office on the esplanade near the ferry terminal. Check here for times of ferry crossings. Boats normally leave every half hour.

Once in Ayamonte, make your own way around. There are no great bargains here, but plenty of Spanish souvenirs and places serving *paella*. If you stay for lunch, take a taxi up to the **Parador Costa de la Luz**, surveying a wide sweep of Spain and Portugal.

19. Beside the Guadiana

Castle at Castro Marim; riverside route to Alcoutim; scenic drive through the Serra do Caldeirado; sundowner at São Brás.

This tour takes you through some of the loveliest river and mountain scenery of the Algarve. Fill up the car before you set off—petrol stations are scarce. And note that the new road alongside the river Guadiana is not marked on most maps. To put the area into perspective, start the day at the hilltop castle of **Castro Marim**. The gate opens at 9am (closed holidays) but there is no need to be here before mid morning (early risers can always breakfast in the border town of Vila Real de Santo António). Climb up to the battlements for good views of the River Guadiana, the natural frontier between Portugal and Spain. To the east you can see the Spanish border town of Ayamonte, to the south Vila Real and just below you the flat saltpans of the region's **nature reserve**, where you might spot a stork or a black-winged stilt. For information on rarer species that come here, ask at the nature reserve information office at the entrance to the castle. The ancient fortress on a hillock to the southwest and what remains of the castle are clues that Castro Marim was once more than a sleepy whitewashed village. The settlement dates back at least to the Phoenicians but the town played its key role in history as the headquarters in 1321 of the Knights of Christ—crucial contributors

Above left: Vila Real de Santo António;
Left and *Below*: Saltpans around Vila Real

in the first phase of the Great Discoveries. Pick up local background information in the **museum** within the castle walls. If shut, ask for the key at the nature reserve office. Leave Castro Marim by noon and take the main EN122 marked to Beja and Mértola. The road climbs through remote rolling hills and over dried-up tributaries of the Guadiana.

Six kilometres beyond Azinhal take the turning right marked Alcoutim and follow the road through cistus-covered hillsides where you are unlikely to see any life other than a herd or two of brown speckled goats. Another 6km and you reach the placid waters of the Gaudiana, with views across to the quiet hills of Andalusia. Slow down to watch peaceful scenes of locals tilling the lush land beside the river or tending to vines and vegetable patches.

At **Foz de Odeleite** the pastel washed houses huddle on the hillside, patios brimming with oleander and geraniums. Follow the road along the river, past fields of corn, groves of olive trees and patches of vines. Stop at **Guerreiros do Rio**, a primitive sleepy riverside village where chickens scratch among the cobbles, and shelter from the heat in makeshift huts. The roads here are just potholed dirt tracks.

Slow down 3km further on, for fine views of the Moorish fortress and village of Sanlúcar de Guadiana on the Spanish side of the river. **Alcoutim**, similarly crowned by castle ruins, soon comes into view on your side of the river. A couple of right turns bring you into the village square. Park here and take the

The Guadiana River

steps between the café and the bank up to the castle for views across the river. Return to the square and walk down to the landing stage where yachts are moored. Look across to Sanlúcar and you might spot a couple of storks nesting on top of the twin belfries of the church. Take lunch any time from noon on at the Café/Restaurant **O Soeiro** (next to the church and waterfront closed weekends). Grab a river view table if you can, watch what's cooking on the brazier outside or see what the locals are tucking into, follow suit and wash it down with a bottle of Real Sassador wine. With time in hand you might find a fisherman with a boat to explore the waters upstream (ask at the tourist office near the landing stage); but make sure you leave Alcoutim by 3.30pm. It is 84 long kilometres to São Brás de Alportel and you will be

Castro do Marim

Leaving Alcoutim, go up the hill and along the EN122-1 till you come to the crossroads. Go straight over for Cachopo. Follow the long stretch of surprisingly straight road over a plateau with rolling hills either side. Eucalyptus trees line the roadside and in spring the white flowers of rock roses and yellow splashes of broom dot the hillsides. Try the village of **Gilões** (marked off the main road 18km beyond the crossroads) to see the last surviving basket weaver. Ask at the whitewashed Centro de Saude on your right as you go into the village and you may see him creating a fine basket or boater. One hat takes him two days to make. Further east and off the main road, stop at **Martim Longo** to see an industrious team of girls hand making sackcloth dolls. You will find them at the back of the blue and white *artesanato* shop as you fork right into the centre of the village. Dolls cost 1,200$ if you buy direct. A few doors on you will find more seamstresses, but this time at machines, making raw silk outfits, for good prices if you buy direct.

A detour south from Martim Longo towards Vaqueiros takes you deeper into the mountains and past the embryonic stages of a safari park for endangered species. A scientific centre, sizable hotel and wild safaris on horseback or by jeep are all in the pipeline. After Martim Longo, the road descends from the plateau, snaking and bumping its way through the pretty rolling landscape to Cachopo. Stop at one of the cafés here, then take the EN124 to Barranco do Velho, a beautiful route with wooded valleys, stepped hillsides, pines and cistus shrubs. At Barranco do Velho take the left fork and follow the road down to São Brás de Alportel in the foothills of the Serra do Caldeirao. Look at all the cork trees with numbers denoting dates of bark stripping. Two kilometres before you reach São Brás, turn left at the sign for the **Pousada de São Brás** (Tel: 089-42305/6). This state run hotel sits on a hill and has beautiful views across the hills, down to the coast. If the place appeals, stay for dinner and try a typically Portuguese dish. Your best bet is the *caldeirada de borrego*, a lamb stew. Less elegant but fun, and a place to meet the Portuguese, is the café-like **Luís dos Frangos** (nicknamed King of the Chickens) in São Brás on the Tavira road. The speciality is barbecued chicken, with salad, chips and cheap wine, served at noisy communal tables.

Sanlucar de Guadiana

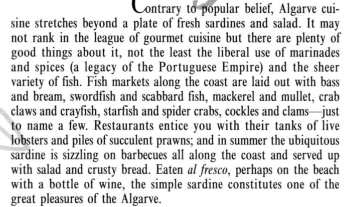

Contrary to popular belief, Algarve cuisine stretches beyond a plate of fresh sardines and salad. It may not rank in the league of gourmet cuisine but there are plenty of good things about it, not the least the liberal use of marinades and spices (a legacy of the Portuguese Empire) and the sheer variety of fish. Fish markets along the coast are laid out with bass and bream, swordfish and scabbard fish, mackerel and mullet, crab claws and crayfish, starfish and spider crabs, cockles and clams—just to name a few. Restaurants entice you with their tanks of live lobsters and piles of succulent prawns; and in summer the ubiquitous sardine is sizzling on barbecues all along the coast and served up with salad and crusty bread. Eaten *al fresco*, perhaps on the beach with a bottle of wine, the simple sardine constitutes one of the great pleasures of the Algarve.

Fish are frequently marinaded in wine, olive oil or herbs, then simply grilled or barbecued. Alternatively they form the basis of wholesome fish soups and casseroles. The Algarve speciality is *amêijoas na cataplana*, a soup/casserole of clams, sausage, ham, garlic, herbs, spices and white wine, served in a *cataplana*—a special domed tin or copper vessel, rather like an old-fashioned pressure cooker. Look out too for *cataplana* dishes with lobster, *tamboril* (monkfish) or clams with pork. The minimum order is usually for two and often ample for three or four. Choose this dish therefore for a long leisurely lunch or dinner. The same applies to *caldeirada*, which is like a French *bouillabaisse* and uses a variety of fish with onions, tomatoes, potatoes and paprika. *Arroz de marisco*, shellfish with rice and spices, is served in huge portions and is usually excellent value for money.

Lobsters are whisked off by restaurateurs before they even reach the market and at about 8,000$ a kilo, they are not cheap. Fresh sea bream is excellent, as is swordfish (*espadarte*) served in steaks and grilled. Beware of 'fresh swordfish' served at any time other than in January and February, when it is caught. It will either be frozen swordfish or mako shark in disguise, which may fool the tourists but not the locals. Confusingly similar in name but entirely different to look at is *peixe espada*, the long, skinny 'scabbard fish' with pointed snout and silvery scales. It is cut in diagonal slices and served grilled.

Less appetising, at least to foreign tastes, are dishes made with *bacalhau,* or dried cod, the most widely available fish dish in Portugal. The grey slabs hanging in shops and market stalls won't entice you, but the locals love this fish and have been eating it since the explorations in Newfoundland began in 1501. As every guide book will tell you, there are as many different ways of cooking dried cod as there are days in the year.

The big ports of Olhão and Portimão for good fish restaurants. Try too the **Rui** restaurant in Silves (Tel: 82-42682, closed Tuesday in winter) and the **O Lotus** in Lagoa (Tel: 82-52098, closed Saturday). Both are excellent for fish, patronised by the Portuguese and not overpriced. Expect to pay around 4,000$ for two for an average three-course meal with wine.

As for meat, good grazing land is virtually non-existent and beef is best avoided. Chicken, may look scrawny but is full of flavour and always a safe bet. Frequently it's marinaded then barbecued (*frango na churrasco*). The ubiquitous 'chicken piri-piri' uses a sauce made from chilli peppers, which can be mild and tangy or as strong as a Vindaloo. Like Indian curry spices, the hot sauce was once used in the African colonies to stop meat from spoiling or hide its bad taste. But don't let that put you off this tasty dish. Monchique has numerous restaurants specialising in piri-piri. Try the **Restaurante Central** in the Caldas de Monchique or the **Paraiso da Montanha** on the Fóia road. Of the various self-styled 'kings of the chickens', the **Luis dos Frangos** on the Tavira road in São Brás de Alportel is one of the best. Unprepossessing and informal, the place does a roaring trade every night in barbecued meats. But the king of the kings of chicken has to be **O Teodosio** in Guia, a town sprawling along the EN125 northwest of Albufeira, whose reputation is built entirely around piri-piri. Expect to pay 1,000$ a head for a meal and half a bottle of Reguengos or Vidiguera wine.

Pork is the alternative to chicken. Portuguese eat pork in all its different forms, from whole roast suckling pig to trotters with coriander. Try *carne de porco com amêijoas*, pork and clams, frequently cooked in a *cataplana*. Lamb may be bony but is good stewed. Kid is either roasted or served in a casserole with onions, tomatoes and potatoes—*cabrito estufado*. This is the speciality of the simple **Restaurant Adega Cova**, Vale d'Eguas in Almansil (Tel: 089-95281, closed Tuesday and holidays), who serve it with their own homemade rosé wine.

Portuguese restaurants tend to be simple, set with paper table-cloths (useful for totting up the *escudos*) and baskets of coarse country bread, saucers of small black olives and perhaps a tin or two of sardine pâté and a little pot of cheese. If that does not suffice as a starter, try the *presunto*, delicious smoked ham (another speciality of Monchique), sometimes served with melon, *gaspacho* (the equivalent of the Spanish soup of the same name) or, on a cool day, *caldo verde*, the most popular soup of Portugal, made with shredded green cabbage and thickened with potatoes and a few slices of sausage.

Along the coast, everyone is catered for—except perhaps the gourmet. Big resorts provide everything from fish and chips to five-star international cuisine. The stars may well denote an elegantly laid table and great service, but are no real indicator of the quality of the food. Prices are markedly higher than those north of the EN125, and menus are nearly always translated into English. Some people claim that the finest restaurant in the Algarve is **La Réserve**, located at Santa Bárbara de Nexe (Tel: 089-91474). The setting is refined and the food (mainly French) is very good, but it's all fiendishly expensive.

Eggs, Sugar and Almonds

The Portuguese sweet tooth is a legacy of the Moors, who introduced almond trees to Portugal and mixed the nuts with egg yolks to make sweetmeats. Several centuries later the enthusiasm for all things sweet was fuelled by the sugar plantations in Madeira. In the 17th and 18th centuries convents were famed for their pastries, and the nuns handed down elusively-named specialities such as as *toucinho do céu* (bacon from heaven) or *barriga de freiras* (nun's belly). Today the Algarve's almonds and figs form the basis of many dozens of desserts and sweets. Marzipan is moulded into myriad shapes, from baby chicks to chessboards. To sample the sweets or fancy cakes and pastries stop at a *pastelaria*. Specialities unique to the Algarve are *Dom Rodrigo* and *Morgado*.

Tarte de amêndoa (almond tart), served at most Portuguese restaurants, is almost invariably good and more inspiring than the selection of ice creams (invariably presented to you on a plastic folder) or the old stand-by, *pudim de flan—crème caramel*. Other than fresh fruit (and occasionally orange tart) few other desserts feature on menus unless you happen to be in an up-market international restaurant.

Wine, Port and Liqueurs

The best thing about Algarve wine is its price. A litre costs as little as 250$. There are two reasons why you don't see a lot of it in restaurants: first, the lack of space between mountains and sea severely limits production; second, the wines' general lack of charm. Try it if you like with a picnic or plate of sardines, but watch out for the effects—13 or 13.5 degrees is quite normal. The biggest producer is **Lagoa,** which bottles mainly red, but also white, rosé and a golden aperitif wine called both **Alfonso** III and **Algar Seco.** You can visit the large wine cooperative in the town of Lagoa, east of Portimão, and watch the labels being glued on by hand. (No tasting apart from groups.) Wines from the **Alentejo,** often served as the *vinho da casa* for as little as 300$/350$, are superb value. Names you are most likely to come across are **Vidigueira** and **Reguengos,** and the full-bodied, dark **Redondo** and **Borba** reds, not unlike Spanish wines. Don't leave the Algarve without trying at least one bottle of

Portugal's more famous reds: the smooth, slightly sweet **Dão**, its up-and-coming rival **Bairrada** (with a growing reputation for still and sparkling whites) and the ruby-red **Colares**, which can be wonderful if aged.

The most characteristic Portuguese wine (far more so than the famous Mateus Rosé) is the light and *pétillant* **Vinho Verde** from the Minho region—a refreshing drink on any occasion. *Verde* refers to the age and not the colour. The wines are drunk very young, usually no later than the spring or summer after the harvest. End your meal with a Portuguese brandy, liqueur or port. The Algarve specialities are the potent **Medronho**, distilled from the berries of the *arbutus unedo* tree, which you see growing in profusion around Monchique, **Algarviana**, made from almonds, and **Branydmel**, a honey-based liqueur. Port is seldom drunk by the locals and is not as cheap as you might imagine. If you are curious, try some of the different types and vintages at the **Cave do**

Vinho do Porto in Rua da Liberdade 23, Albufeira, or at the Artisans' Village on the main EN125 between Alcantarilha and Porches (free wine tasting). White port (*porto branco*), frequently dismissed by wine buffs as being inferior to its more celebrated relative, makes an excellent aperitif when served chilled. Go for the drier, paler makes. The exotic dessert wine **Madeira**, produced on the island of the same name, is the only wine to be heated in a special oven or *estufa* before being consumed. There are four basic types, from light and dry to rich and sweet.

Cafés, Snacks and Picnics

In Portuguese cafés look for the day's dishes scribbled up on blackboards. These may be a plate of sardines, a mixed salad, a nourishing stew and a simple omelette. After a lot of dew or rain you may see a notice on bars and cafés for snails or *caracois,* which the locals eat with lager. Coffee is invariably good. Ask for *uma bica* (espresso), *um garoto* (small with milk), or *um galao* (large with milk). For a snack or or main meal you can also try a *cervejaria*, somewhere between a café and a restaurant, or a *marisqueira,* which specialises in seafood. Whether self-catering or preparing a picnic, markets are invariably the best source. They are open 8am to 12.30–1pm. Choose cold meats from the hanging rows of *chouricos* (sausages), *presunto* (smoked ham) and fresh fruits. Typical cheeses are *Queijo da Serra*, made from ewes' milk and matured in wood cellars, or *cabreiro*, goats' cheese. Larger markets sell bread; otherwise go to a local bakery for large crusty rolls, rough country loaves or bread flavoured with pork.

Nightlife

Twenty years ago nightlife in the Algarve amounted to no more than a glass of wine or Medronho in a little *adega* or, at its liveliest, an evening of music, song and dance at a local *festa*. With the advent of tourism came the inevitable invasion of discos and nightclubs. With local wine and lager at giveaway prices, late night bars and pubs began to flourish—at least along the coast. Today, nightlife consists of dozens of discos, three casinos, various cabarets and occasional folklore and *fado* nights. Prices are no longer cheap. Unless you are a single woman (who may be admitted free) expect to pay anything from 1,000$ to 5,000$ entrance to a nightclub, first drink included.

Discos The hottest spot is Albufeira, which throbs to the beat of discos until the early hours of the morning. The majority are undistinguished, with earsplitting music, loud tourists or hot-blooded Portuguese in the inevitable pursuit of foreign female talent. Discos go in and out of fashion with remarkable rapidity. The latest 'in' place, recently opened, is **Kadoc**, on the outskirts of Vilamoura, a vast disco with an open air terrace. Another trendy new spot is **Locomia** at Santa Eulalia, east of Albufeira, which seems to lure the young, well-heeled Portuguese. Entrance is free; drinks are 1,000$ a shot. The key feature here is a giant champagne bottle, suspended from the ceiling, which intermittently spews forth a great stream of foam, filling the dance floor well above waist level and providing a good excuse for shedding a garment.

Further east, at Quinta do Lago, you can rub shoulders with the jet set at the **Pátio** night club—providing you are willing to pay a minimum of 5,000$. There is no entrance charge; the bill is surreptitiously settled as you leave. Other good bets for music and ambience are **Horta 2** (between Portimão and Odiáxere), **Phoenix** in Lagos, **Trigonometria** in Quinta do Lago and **Privé** in Praia da Luz. In any disco be prepared to wait until 1am for things to hot up.

Casinos

Lay your bets at **Vilamoura, Monte Gordo** or **Alvor**. Passports or ID cards are essential and men are expected to wear jackets. Gaming rooms open in the early evening for Roulette, Blackjack, French Bank and slot machines. The entrance charge is around 1,000$. Added incentives are three-course meals and (mediocre) live performances, starting at around 5,000$. Gaming rooms close at 3 or 4am.

Cabaret

The showplace for international glitter and glamour is **Michael's** at Montechoro (Tel: 89-55997), 3kms east of Albufeira. The price of 4,500$ includes *Folies Bergères* style shows, live music, entertainment, dancing and dinner. Book direct or through agencies and hotel receptions.

Fado

Lamentations of lost loves, lovers crossed or the forces of destiny are all characteristic themes of the Portuguese *fado*. Sung by professionals, these chants are plangent, haunting and intensely moving. To the unattuned ear they can sound strange and monotonous, hence the jollification of traditional *fado* for the benefit of tourists in the Algarve. Authentic *fado* has its roots in Lisbon (city folk sang songs of love; country and coast folk of the weather, crops and sea) and it is in the cafés and restaurants of the *Bairro Alto* quarter of the capital that you are more likely to hear the real thing. If you are keen to see a performance in the Algarve, consult local, English-language magazines, and newspapers such as the *Algarve Gazette* and the *Algarve News* for the various venues along the coast. The **Sol e Mar Hotel** in the centre of Albufeira, the **O Muralho**, at the top of the Rua Infante de Sagres in Lagos and the **Hotel Eva** in Faro are three of the main venues, all tourist-orientated. Alternatively, you may just be lucky and catch some gifted *fado* singer giving an impromptu performance in a village restaurant.

Folk Dancing

The regional folk dances are colourful affairs performed with vigour and enthusiasm, but rarely on a professional level. The groups are formed in local villages and most of the dancers work in the daytime as maids, labourers, builders etc. Local publications will give you details of folk dancing venues (the **Fonte Pequena Folklore Centre** in the hillside village of Alte [see Itinerary 10] is one of the main places). Or you can see dancers at fairs in many towns and villages in the Algarve. The traditional folk dance of the region is the *corridinho*, a lively and joyful country dance despite the fact that the dancers wear black costumes.

Shopping

The best buys are handicrafts: wickerwork, ceramics, embroidery, rugs, copper, brass, wrought iron, woodwork and leather. Along the coast, where souvenir shops and stalls do a roaring trade in cheap baskets from China, you are unlikely to catch a glimpse of that dying breed, the Algarve artisan. Weavers transforming sisal fibres into baskets and hampers, craftsmen beating copper and brass, and ladies lace making at their doorways are fast disappearing. Inland, however, you will still occasionally find surviving artisans proucing the genuine articles. (See Itineraries 11 and 19.)

Check in local English-language magazines for the dates of weekly markets and fairs. These are large colourful affairs, where you can pick up reasonably priced pottery, basketry, linen and lace. The big gipsy markets sell everything from fresh mountain cheeses to old liquor stills and pots of snake oil. The *artesanato* stalls dotted all along the EN125 are fun for browsing.

Antiques

For sheer amusement try the **Casa da Papagaio**, Rua 25 de Abril in Lagos, stacked with priceless Portuguese antiques and dusty religious artefacts which look as though they should be in a museum. Ask to see inside the locked rooms beyond the main shop. (If you are sufficiently interested they will show you their second shop in Lagos, normally closed to the public.) Their other branch is in Portimão, in Rua Santa Isabel. Also in Portimão try **A Tralha** in Rua Vasco da Gama, for antiques and Madeira embroideries). Or, for something entirely different, the roadside *artesanato* on the EN125

Leather working

(soon after the Loulé turn-off if you are travelling east–west) sell an amusing collection of old ploughs, cart wheels, liquor stills and other rural bygones.

Basketry

Baskets range from the cheap imported variety to those that have taken a local two days to make. To see Algarve weavers at work turn off the EN125 at Boliqueime to the road for Loulé and (dependent on time of year and day) you may well see them busily working by the roadside. Buy direct. See also Itinerary 19, which takes you through mountain villages where a few basket-makers and other craftsmen still survive.

Ceramics

Arguably the best buy, though also the most cumbersome to carry home, are ceramics. The choice is endless, from roosters, mini-chimneys, snails and vine leaves to Greek and Roman-style *amphorae*. Pictorial *azulejos*, the glazed Portuguese tiles, make attractive gifts, though the old ones are over priced.

The potteries at Porches, sprawled along the EN125, are the best source for sheer variety. Try **Casa Algarve** or **Porches Pottery**, which competes with its large range of floral-patterned hand painted *majolica* and has the added advantage of an inviting bar *in situ*. Traditions here have been handed down over the centuries—at least until the 1960s, when metal and plastic took over and becoming a potter became *infra dig*. In 1968 an Irishman, Patrick Swift saw a way of reviving a dying industry by decorating plain pottery and selling it to the tourists beginning to invade the Algarve. The idea took off and the place is now run by his son-in-law, Roger Metcalfe. The *majolica* is all hand painted (you can see the girls at work) and patterns are all variations on traditional designs. Opening hours: Monday to Friday all day, Saturday 10–1pm, 4–6pm (7pm in summer).

The choice of ceramics is complex. Cheapest is the glazed Algarve terracotta pottery bordered with a white floral line and widely used by the locals. But keep a look-out too for pottery from other regions of Portugal. Coimbra's hand painted pottery depicting animals and

and birds in floral settings is notable. Then there is the distinctive and decorative Alentejo pottery, often illustrated with flowers, fish or simple scenes from daily life. Also, consider picking up Leiria pottery with its bright, bold designs (usually fish and flowers) and

Coppersmith

the liking of those with designer taste. For an unusual selection of antique-styled Portuguese earthenware (in addition to modern designs) don't miss the **Infante D Henrique House** in Rua Cândido dos Reis, Albufeira.

Copper and Brass

If you happen to be strolling around the Rua 9 de Abril or Rua da Barbaça in Loulé, you are still likely to hear the beating of brass and copper. Craftsmen here work in tiny workshops and the nearby shops are full of their pots and pans. Look out for old liquor stills—a really unusual buy—and *cataplanas* (try your hand at cooking Algarve specialities at home) sold at *artesanato* stalls on the EN125 road side, for example, between Olhão and Tavira.

Crystal

The old Portuguese art of glass-making still survives. Today the big name is Atlantis, a Portuguese full lead crystal. **O Aquario** in Rua Vasco da Gama, Portimão has top quality crystal and also sells Vista Alegre, the finest porcelain in Portugal.

Embroidery, Lace and Weaving

'Where there are nets, there is lace' goes the local saying. You certainly see plenty of it along the coast but not a lot is handmade these days. Good buys in shops and stalls are colourful heavy bedspreads, rugs and curtains from the Alentejo, either with simple patterns or ethnic scenes. Look out too for hand woven carpets from Arraiolos, north of Evora. The best venue for these is **Arraiolos**, Rua Dr Teófilo Braga, next to the Town Hall in Portimão, who make to order and ship abroad.

Look too in markets for woven mats or rugs, striped, patterned or plain, and selling for as little as 500$.

To see locals weaving try the first tower on your left as you go into the castle at Silves where women work at looms making tablecloths, bedspreads, etc. Orders can be taken and shipped to your home. Villagers still crochet in their spare time but rarely for the benefit of tourists. Their immaculately made bedspreads with fine patterns are often tucked away in trunks and cupboards. The only way of buying direct is to ask in the villages who embroiders or crochets: *Onde posso encontrar uma senhora que saba fazer colchas e toalhas de mesa em crochet?*

Souvenir hunting

Food and Wine

Tio José in Praça da República, Portimão, boasts the 'largest selection of Portuguese port, wines and brandies'. The excellent Bairrada wines are good travellers. Good years are 1970, '74, '75, '78, '81, '82, '84 and 1985 (the last two should be laid down). Avoid the duty-free drink shops unless you want to buy foreign spirits. Markets are a good source for cheeses, hams, sausages and fresh food generally. Sweets made of almonds, marzipan and figs are sold everywhere and make an attractive gift.

Jewellery

One of the best buys is Marcasite, a legacy of the Moors. Small rings start for as little as 850$. Look also for filigree work, an old Portuguese craft. Pliable silver and gold wire is still fashioned into shapes such as birds, flowers and other delicate designs. For imaginative designs in jewellery try the following shops: **Mogodor**, Rua Gil Eanes, Lagos; **Terracotta**, Praça Luís de Camões, Lagos; and **Stárte**, Rua Guilherme Gomes Fernandes, No 26, Tavira (behind the cinema).

Leather

There are some good buys if you are prepared to shop around. Cheap bags in markets and stalls start at about 1,500$, but expect to pay 20,000$ for a top designer creation in a boutique. For shoes try the shops in Loulé, **Charles Jourdan at St. James** in Portimão (Rua Santa Isabel) or Albufeira (Av Eduardo Rios), for classical Parisian designs at Portuguese prices. Other worthwhile sources are **Malas Artigos de Viagem** on the corner of Rua Direita and Vasco da Gama in Portimão (huge range of handbags); **Via Gama**, Av Dr Sá Carneiro, Albufeira; and **Oberon** and **António Manuel Boutique** (soft leather jackets) in the Rua de Santo António in Faro.

Woollens

The best sources for chunky woollen cardigans and jumpers, patterned or plain, are (surprisingly) the stalls outside Sagres fortress and Cape St Vincent. Fisherman's jumpers and woolly socks are excellent buys; so are hand dyed cotton jumpers. **NB** See Itinerary 4 for shopping in Portimão.

Antique liquor still

85

Sport

Sports enthusiasts are spoilt for choice. The Algarve has all the ingredients for an active holiday: all year sunshine, fine beaches for water sports, a choice of resorts with their own sports centres and a hinterland ribboned with some of the finest golf courses in Europe. The seawater is choppy for water sports novices but you can often practise on nearby lagoons.

Golf Not surprisingly the Algarve promotes itself as a golfer's paradise. There are 12 courses, eight of them championship, and there are more in the pipeline. But spiralling green fees and the incessant demand for preferential tee times, especially from May to October, are already putting some players off the game. At the exclusive new **San Lorenzo** the only hope of membership is to buy a plot, put down 5,000,000$ (£20,000) membership fee and 250,000$ (£1,000) every year! Green fees at the top venues are 10,000$, hence the courses are becoming more and more the domain of the international jet set.

If you are serious about playing, plan your trip with care. The only way to guarantee preferential tee times and secure green fee discounts is either to stay in a hotel affiliated with the course or to rent a villa on the fringes of the fairways. In the summer months try to arrange your games for early morning or late afternoon to avoid the intense midday heat.

Main Courses QUINTA DO LAGO (Tel: 089-394529/ 394782); Green fees: 10,000$. Fifty-four holes—and more on the way. The most famous and probably the most exclusive course in the Algarve. The 1,500 sprinklers keep the greens in immaculate condition and the tees have been compared to bowling greens. Very scenic terrain with pine woods, lakes and wildlife. Trees and water (from fresh and saltwater pools) are the main hazards.

PENINA (Tel: 082-415415); Green fees: 7,500$. Eighteen-hole championship course and two nine-hole courses. The

longest established course in the Algarve, designed by Henry Cotton. Beautifully landscaped course, lush greens with woods and strategically placed lakes and streams. Notorious short par-three 13th where, in 1986 dredgers in the adjoining lake uncovered around 20,000 lost balls. Five-star facilities include the Hotel Penina, tennis and pool.

SAN LORENZO (Tel: 089-396522); Green fees: 10,000$. Eighteen-hole championship course. New and very exclusive, owned by THF. Scenically similar to Quinta do Lago. To secure a game you have to stay either at the nearby Dona Filipa Hotel, the Penina Hotel or the new San Lorenzo Hotel currently under construction, or own or rent one of the smart new villas on the 2,000-acre estate at Quinta do Lago.

PINE CLIFFS (Tel: 089-50787); Recently opened but incomplete luxury golf and country club featuring a par-32 nine-hole golf course, five-star Sheraton Hotel, large pool, villas and apartments, overlooking ravines and beach.

VALE DO LOBO (Tel. 089-394444); Green fees: 6,500$. Three nine-hole courses. Another one designed by Henry Cotton. The seventh hole on the Yellow Course, stretching 192m (210yds) over two ravines, is the most photographed in Europe. Spectacular sea views from the Yellow and Orange courses.

VILAMOURA I (Tel 089-313652); Green fees: 5,500$. Eighteen-hole course. Located among pine forests, with sea views. Venue of various major championships.

VILAMOURA II (Tel: 089-315562); Green fees: 5,500$. Eighteen-hole course. Opened in 1976 but recently redesigned with nine new holes. Spectacular sea views from first nine holes; back nine through umbrella pines.

VILAMOURA III. Newly opened 18-hole course with luxury clubhouse.

PALMARES (Tel: 62961/62953); Green fees: 4,700$. Eighteen-hole course near Lagos. This underrated centre features undulating terrain with some spectacular views of sea and hills. This fabulous venue is famous for the Almond Blossom Tournament.

PARQUE DE FLORESTA (Tel: 082-65333–5); Green fees: 4,000$. Set in rolling hills above Salema about 16kms west of Lagos, the course offers a real challenge. A residential complex and hotel are planned.

Driving Ranges

BALAIA VILLAGE, near Albufeira. 50-bay driving range, open six days a week.

CLUB BARRINGTON, Vale do Lobo. 29-bay, two-tiered driving range, open seven days a week.

Riding

You can ride across dunes and lagoons or trek in the hillsides. There are excellent riding opportunities and several schools, some English run. The superior stables at **Quinta do Lago** (Pinetrees Tel: 089-394369) are run just like an English riding school. There are pony rides, treks, hacks, beach rides and trips into the Ludo valley. Other ranches include the **Centro Hípico at Vilamoura** (Tel: 089-32535), **Vista Mar Riding Centre** at Burgau (Tel: 082-65234), **Centro Hípico O Cangalho** (12km from Lagos, picnic rides in the mountains and Algarve cart rides—Tel: 082-67218), the **Riding Centre**, Vale de Ferro, Mexilhoeira Grande (Tel: 082-96444/3—over 30 different treks originating from a scenic ranch in the foothills of Monchique); and the **Aldeia das Acoteias**, Praia da Falésia (Tel: 089-66267).

Water Sports

Wind surfing schools with instruction and board hire are located all along the coast. Real surfing is best along the west coast. Water skiing is usually only available in the larger resorts and only in high season. The main marina is at Vilamoura, where you can rent yachts and motor boats (Tel: 089-314818), but there are plenty of other places for renting boats including Lagos (at the Sailing Club), Vila Real, Tavira and Faro. A good spot for beginners, either for wind surfing, water skiing or sailing, is the calm expanse of water on the *Barragem do Arade* near Silves. Anyone interested in scuba diving should contact Atlantic Diving Algoz (Tel 082-55301). This is a British run centre offering introductory and full courses, sea and shore dives.

Paragliding and Microlighting

LAGOS AERODROME (Tel: 082-62906). Microlighting trips: 6,500$ (seven mins), 9,000$ (15 mins), 11,500$ (30 mins). Lessons available for both microlighting and paragliding. Another good spot for paragliding is the **Clube da Quinta,** Quinta do Lago, with excellent views of the Ria Formosa nature reserve.

Tennis

There are courts all along the coast. The main centre is the **Roger Taylor Tennis Club** at Vale do Lobo, (Tel: 089-394779) with 12 courts, restaurant and pool. Instruction is available. Other centres along the coast are the Rock Garden Sports Centre, Vilamoura (Tel: 089-33899), the Vilamoura Tennis Club (Tel: 089-313612), the Aldeamento Túristico Montechoro at Albufeira, (Tel: 089-52651/2/3), and the Burgau Sports Centre (Tel: 082-65350).

Fishing

For Big Game Fishing see Itinerary 5. Alternatively, try fishing from beaches, rocks, jetties or in the inland reservoirs. Equipment can be hired in most resorts. Fishermen occasionally take tourists out in their boats, either for serious fishing or a tour of the coastline and grottoes. Look out for notices on the beaches.

Water Parks

Huge water chutes, which resemble giant coloured snakes are the most eye-catching features along the EN125. Prices range from 1,250$–2,300$ (adult) and 750$–1,300$ (child).

THE BIG ONE, Alcantarilha, on the EN125. Large park with exciting slides and rides: corkscrew, raging rapids, flying carpets, wave pool, crazy leap.

ATLANTICO, Quatro Estradas (between Quarteira and Loulé). Acapulco high-diving team in high season.

WILD WATERS, Montechoro Park, Albufeira. Almost a mile of slides and rides; giant flumes and Australian tube slides; Algarve's largest pool. Local transport free.

SLIDE & SPLASH, Lagoa (Estombar Road). Four main slides plus double corkscrew, whirlpool, waterfall, river ride, etc.

Sports Clubs

CLUB BARRINGTON, Vale do Lobo (Tel: 089-394444). Five-star club with squash, gym, sauna, jacuzzi, swimming pool, cricket, etc.

ROCK GARDEN, Vilamoura (Tel:089-314740). One-, three- and five-day memberships available for squash, tennis, snooker, swimming.

BURGAU SPORTS CENTRE, English run club with tennis, squash, swimming, aerobics, and five-a-side football.

BULLFIGHTING

In 1799 the Portuguese Count of Arcos, one of the more foolhardy matadors of his day, was fatally injured in the ring. As a result the King of Portugal, deeming bullfighting to be an all too dangerous sport, declared that in future the bull's horns would be padded and the animal always leave the ring alive. Since then Portuguese bullfights have been less violent affairs, with all the emphasis on the skill and elegance involved in taunting and subduing rather than slaying the bull. If this sounds preferable to the Spanish *corrida*, bear in mind that the bulls are often injured and usually slaughtered shortly after the fight.

The season lasts from May until October. Fights take place on Saturday at 5.30pm. Eye-catching posters on walls throughout the Algarve will announce any imminent fights, or you can find the dates in local magazines. Tickets may be bought at hotels or at the ring, and prices vary according to the position of the seats.

Bullfighting enthusiasts who have seen a fight in the Ribatejo, breeding ground of the best bulls, claim that Algarve fights are tame affairs aimed entirely at the tourists. This may be true but tourists who go tend to enjoy the spectacle for its sheer entertainment and (comparative) lack of gore, regardless of the quality of the bulls or fighters. The fact that the bull is continuously active throughout the fight (as opposed to the Spanish *corrida*, where the *picadores* can severely weaken the animal) makes it a lively, exciting and dangerous event right through to the very end.

The fight begins with the *toureiro* (matador), decked out in flamboyant 18th-century costume and brandishing his red cape to bait the bull. Next to appear are the *cavaleiros*, horsemen on stallions, who stab the bull's shoulders with *farpas* (darts) as it charges. The final act involves eight acrobatic *forcados* who run in to challenge the animal. The leader, or *londroal*, goads the bull and, as it charges, hurls himself between its horns, while the rest of the team wrestle with the beast and bring it down to the ground. This *coup de grace* is known as the *pegas*.

Calendar of Special Events

The Portuguese have a passion for public holidays, fairs and festivals, and the southerners are no exception. Dozens of towns and villages in the Algarve celebrate the local patron saint's day with parades, fireworks and plenty of merriment in the form of song and dance. Some are strictly religious, while others have become events aimed primarily at the tourists. Either way they are colourful, earthy events, well worth sampling if they happen to coincide with your visit. To witness the more ethnic of the 'feast' days, seek out celebrations in the small-

er villages where locals will insist you join in the merriment. Local tourist offices provide regularly updated leaflets on events throughout the region.

January

'Charolas': Between New Year and Twelfth Night groups of singers and musicians, holding up banners with ribbons and flowers, roam through the streets of towns and villages singing traditional seasonal songs. The New Year's Day speciality, endorsing the Portuguese passion for sweet and sticky cakes, is a sugary bun not unlike a doughnut.

Late February/Early March

Carnival is the year's big event. Celebrations begin four Saturdays before Shrove Tuesday with dancing in carnival costume, and culminate in three days of street merriment. It's a time when everyone lets off steam, pranksters throw rotten eggs and flour and neighbours say what they really think about each other. Largest and liveliest is the carnival at **Loulé** with its procession of colourful floats, marching bands and dancing groups. Deeply rooted in paganism, carnival traditionally celebrates the end of winter, and in some smaller villages you can still witness the mock 'burial' of winter. A 'corpse', either in the form of a real person or an effigy of death, is carried through the village streets, while black-clad villagers 'in mourning' follow behind. The 'corpse' is taken to the churchyard and ceremoniously buried or burned. Once the event is complete, winter is finally over, joy resumes and wild celebrations begin.

March/April

Easter is celebrated with religious processions, typically led by a priest swinging a censer of burning herbs, and followers strewing symbolic flowers in the streets. Annual processions are held in **Faro, Alcantarilha, Algoz** and **Lagoa**. **São Brás de Alportel** has a colourful festival on Easter Sunday when the streets are strewn with flowers. The second Sunday after Easter the *Romaria e Festa da Mae Soberana* at **Loulé** is a strange and unique folk pilgrimage, intermingling pagan and Christian elements.

Anniversary of the 1974 Revolution: This event, on 25 April, commemorates, the end of the dictatorship era of Salazaron.

May

May Day is celebrated by folk festivals in **Albufeira, Guia, Paderne, Alcoutim, Odeleite, Estômbar** and **Alte**. Join in in the festivities, see folk dance competitions and buy from stalls selling local handicrafts and symbolic bunches of flowers. **Alte** is the main venue.

The Festa da Pinha (Pine Festival), on 1, 2 and 3 May in **Estói**, dates back to the times when farmers travelled to the Alentejo by mule to trade. If they returned safely with the traded goods, unscathed by bandits, the occasion was celebrated by feasting and drinking in the forests. Wine and beer still flow, along with barbecued chicken, dancers, accordianists and guitarists.

The Festa da Espiga in **Salir** is an old farming folk festival, held in the second week of May, celebrating the fertility of the soil and its abundant crops. Floats are traditionally decorated in green (symbolising crops) and red (symbolising poppies). The procession is followed by fireworks and folk dancing. Don't be surprised if you are handed a spray of plants—each one has a special significance.

May/June

The Algarve Music Festival now draws international as well as Portuguese participants. Concerts and recitals are held at the Cathedral in **Silves**, the parish church in **Albufeira** and other ecclesiastical venues with good acoustics. There are also ballet performances.

June

Santos Populares (Saints Day) is traditionally a time when the locals 'come out' and make merry with dancing, music, food and drink. Streets throughout the Algarve are decorated with banners. In some villages rosemary is burnt and children jump over the open fires—probably dating back to pagan initiation rites.

National Day, celebrated on 10 June, marks the anniversary of the death of Luís de Camóes, Portugal's great poet.

July

The Feira do Carmo, is a major festival held in Faro. This fair is a good source for local handicrafts.

The Beer Festival in **Silves** is a predictably merry event, with brass bands and folk dancers, held in the third week in July.

August

The Sardine and Seafood Festival at **Olhão** makes the most of the fact that Portugese sardines are now at their fattest and tastiest.

September

National Folklore Festivals, with folk dancing, *fado* and folklore music, are held throughout the Algarve and provide a good opportunity to buy local handicrafts.

October

The International Algarve Car Rally, featuring Portuguese and European championships is held at a different place each year.

The Feira de Santa Iria is a large fair/festival held in **Faro.**

Republic Day: This Bank Holiday commemorates 5 October, 1910, when the monarchy was finally overthrown.

2 November

All Souls' Day is taken very seriously. After prayers the women, traditionally clad in black, leave the church laden with chrysanthemums to place on the graves of their loved ones. The chrysanthemum, which blooms in winter, is seen by many as the symbol of life in the darkness of death.

25 December

Christmas Day is traditionally a low-key, strictly religious affair. Only in recent years has Santa come down the chimney. *Bacalhau a Brás*, a dish of cod, egg and potato, is traditionally eaten on Christmas Eve; fowl or mutton on Christmas Day. 'Christmas Cake' is a type of bread topped with preserved fruit. Custom dictates that whomever gets the slice with the broad bean has to provide the cake next year.

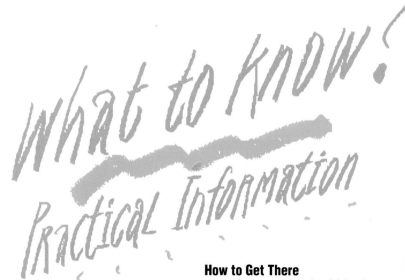
What to Know?
Practical Information

Climate—When to Go

The Algarve has the best of both worlds: pleasantly mild in winter and not too hot in summer. Temperatures rarely rise above 31°—at least this was the case until the last two years when they soared to 38°. The hottest months are July and August. The ideal time to go is in spring, before the temperatures soar and the madding crowds arrive. To see the almond trees in blossom you need to go as early as late January or February, when temperatures are still at their coolest. In April and May the countryside is lush and green with a profusion of wild flowers. Later on the landscape looks very parched and barren. Autumns are mild but the last three Novembers have been very wet. Official records state that the Algarve averages 3,000 hours of sunshine each year—more than the Costa Brava, Majorca or the French Riviera.

The temperature of the sea tends to be quite a lot cooler than that of the Mediterranean. The official temperature of the water in summer is 21°–22°, but it feels colder. The west coast waters are the coolest; as you go east the waters warm up by degree or two.

How to Get There

TAP Air Portugal and British Airways operate in tandem a regular service from Heathrow direct to Faro. British Airways also has a daily flight to Faro from Gatwick throughout the summer. Countless charter flights operate from London and various regional airports. Costs of these are far cheaper than scheduled services. Charter flights are conditional on your staying a Saturday night and scheduled flights punish you severely if you don't (BA high season Superpex £153; unconditional fare £356). From New York there are flights to Lisbon most days of the week, with connecting flights to Faro.

The train journey from the UK is long and more expensive than the cost of a charter flight—assuming you are over 26. Going by car takes from two to three days. Faro is 2,250kms (1,395 miles) from the Channel ports, but you can reduce journey time substantially by taking the Plymouth to Santander ferry crossing.

From Lisbon there are frequent flights to Faro; also a rail service to Faro and Lagos.

Visas and Passports

Visitors from the EC, US and Australia need only a passport for visits of up to three months. EC residents may use excursion passes or visitors' passports.

Driving Licenses
EC driving licenses or international driving licenses are valid in Portugal.

Vaccinations
No vaccinations are officially required for visitors from the EC or USA.

Money Matters
The Portuguese monetary unit is the *escudo*, divided into 100 *centavos*. The *escudo* is written like a dollar sign ($) *after* the amount, hence 80$50 is 80 *escudos, 50 centavos*. Bank note denominations are 10,000$, 5,000$ 1000$, 500$ and 100$. There are coins of 100$, 50$, 25$, 10$, 2$50, 1$ and 50 *centavos*, the last two almost worthless. Working in such big sums can be confusing. If you are English it helps to think of 1,000$ as £4.

Travellers' cheques are the safest way to carry money and rates are more favourable than they are for cash. Banks charge a high commission rate on every transaction, so it is cheaper to change one large amount rather than lots of small ones. Eurocheques with a card are widely accepted.

Nearly all restaurants and shops will change travellers' cheques for you, which is useful when the banks are shut, but the commission they take is nearly always higher than the official bank rate. Major credit cards are accepted by the majority of larger hotels, restaurants and shops. Main garages along the EN125 take Visa, but the majority still accept only cash.

Clothing
Take light clothes in summer, plus a jersey or two for cool evenings. In winter it is wise to take a warm jacket or anorak, though during the daytime you are likely to need no more than a jersey, if that. Casinos and some luxury restaurants prefer men to wear jacket and tie. Elsewhere, casual wear is the norm. Whatever time of year you go, remember to take sunglasses.

Electrical Equipment
The supply is 220/240 volts AC. Plugs have two round pins and most British and American appliances will need an adaptor. The larger hotels will usually supply these.

ON ARRIVAL

Customs Regulations
You may bring as much currency into the country as you wish but any amount exceeding 40,000$ must be declared.

Transport from the Airport
The airport is 7km west of Faro and the journey by car to the centre takes about 15 minutes. Taxis cost roughly 700$. Buses (80$) run roughly every hour in the daytime in summer, but services at weekends are more limited. Car hire companies, both international and local, have branches at the airport (see Getting Around). In summer the journey to Albufeira by car takes about 45mins; Sagres, at the far westerly tip, 2hrs to 2hrs 30mins. On a really bad day in high season it could take you longer, but the new dual carriageway being built from the Spanish border to Vila do Bispo will cut down the time.

GETTING AROUND

By Car

To cover the itineraries which form the core of this book you have no choice but to rent a car. If you are pleasantly surprised by the car hire rates (currently among the cheapest in Europe) you may not be so pleased by the price of petrol. To fill a small car costs at least 5,000$/£20.

It is normally cheaper to reserve a car before you leave home, though the recent downswing in tourism in the Algarve has resulted in a lot of local firms offering very cheap on-the-spot deals. The international car hire companies are inevitably more expensive than the smaller local firms and not always worth the extra. A reliable Portuguese company is **Auto Cerro**, who have a branch at the airport. To hire a car you must be over 23 and have had a license for at least a year. Valid British, EC, American or international licenses are accepted. Always check whether rates include tax.

Driving in the Algarve is not without its hazards. The national highway, the EN125, which extends the length of the region, came out in a recent survey as the second most dangerous road in Europe. The main hazard is the un-predictability of Portuguese drivers: who overtake on blind bends, fail to indicate and generally lack any sort of road etiquette. Some of the locals behind the wheel have never passed or even taken a test, so watch out! Dangers at night are bicycles without lights, horse drawn carts and inconspicuous locals dressed in black. On secondary roads watch out for flocks of sheep or goats wandering aimlessly across the road and beware of potholes.

Finding your way along the coast presents no problems. The EN125, running more or less parallel, goes all the way from the Spanish border to Vila do Bispo in the far west, with side roads going south to resorts and beaches. The signing along here (as opposed to inland) is fairly efficient. For most of the way the road is two-lane only and in some sections (notably west of Lagos) it is poorly surfaced, narrow and more akin to a minor road. However, the new dual carriageway, currently under construction, will take a lot of traffic off the EN125 and speed up journeys considerably. Estimated date for completion of the stretch from the Spanish border to Albufeira is 1991; the remainder by 1992.

Filling up a car with petrol is easy if you are anywhere near the EN125, but petrol stations are sparse in some inland regions. Always use Super.

Before you set out on the itineraries it is useful to know that a *praia* is a beach and a *praca* or *largo* is a square.

Rules of the Road

Speed limits are 120km/hr on motorways, 90km/hr on other roads and 60km/hr in built-up areas. Keep to the right and give priority to vehicles entering from the right unless you see a STOP sign. Safety belts are compulsory outside built-up areas. Drinking and driving is against the law and the limit of alcohol is the same as in the UK.

By Bus

A comprehensive network run by the state owned *Rodoviária Nacional* covers the whole region, including tiny villages. Fares are very reasonable. For long journeys it is far quicker to use one of the express services run by private companies, but you will need to buy a ticket in advance. Various express coach services run to Lisbon from Faro, Albufeira, Portimão, Lagos and other main centres.

By Train

A train service operates from Vila Real de Santo António in the east to Lagos in the west, stopping off at Tavira, Olhão, Faro, Albufeira and Silves. It is very cheap and quite an amusing way to see some of inland Algarve, but not if you are in a hurry.

Taxis

Portuguese cabs are black with green roofs, and you can usually find them in the centres of towns and resorts. Elsewhere you will have to call for one. Fares are reasonable by European standards though they tend to be a lot higher south of the EN125.

Bike Hire

Hiring a motor bike has its hazards. There are numerous accidents involving both locals and tourists along the EN125. Driving along potholed secondary roads can be dodgy too. Bicycles may be hired in main resorts but cycling inland up hills can be hot and gruelling.

By Foot

Getting around towns on foot is facilitated by pedestrianized shopping streets. There are some lovely coastal and inland walks, best done off-season or at either end of a hot summer's day. Other than the walks suggested in the itineraries the following are well worth trying: *Barragem da Bravura*, 14km north of Lagos, a large unspoilt reservoir surrounded by wood-ed hills; the *Barragem do Arade*, a smaller reservoir northeast of Silves, with beautiful walks all round; the verdant hills of Monchique, where temperatures are noticeably cooler than along the coast; and the west coast, which provides wonderful and very bracing cliff top walks.

Maps

The Bartholomew Clyde Leisure Map of the Algarve is the easiest to follow, but the far north of the region is only covered by an inset map and the new roads are not yet marked. The most up-to-date is the touring map of the Algarve published by the *Automóvel Club de Portugal*. Free local maps, available at tourist offices and car hire companies are only sufficient if you are concentrating on the coast.

Ordnance survey maps of the region, available at McCarta, 122 King's Cross Road, London WC1 (£3.95 each), are not as accurate as their British equivalents.

WHERE TO STAY

The bulk of accommodation along the coast comprises self-catering villas or apartments. Standards are high by European standards and some of the villas are the height of luxury with marble furnishings, manicured gardens and pools. Some of the most luxurious accommodation lies on the fringes of golfing fairways.

The range of hotels starts with the simple family run *pensão* (pension) or *residencial* and culminates in five-star luxury. In between and well worth seeking out is the privately run four-star *estalagem*, or inn, which tends to have fewer facilities than a hotel but far more Portuguese character; or the *albergaria*, which is very similar to an *estalagem*. State run *pousadas*, equivalent to the Spanish *paradors*, are thin on the ground in the Algarve. There

is one on a hill north of São Brás de Alportel and a rather superior one on the cliff tops in Sagres.

Hotels are graded from one to five stars, but prices are no longer state controlled. You may find that a three-star pension may be a lot more appealing and possibly cheaper than a hotel of one star. In high season along the coast, prices of rooms can almost double. If you arrive without a booking ask to see the room before you take it. This is considered quite normal practice. Any hotel with three or more stars will probably have its own pool or at least easy access to a beach.

If all official accommodation is taken, enquire locally or at the tourist office about rooms to let in private houses. Staying in a simple room with a local family will cut your costs and improve your Portuguese.

The following are hotels singled out either for their Portuguese character, location, charm or general ambience. The list is be no means comprehensive. In high season expect to pay anything from 2,000$–4,500$ in a pension for a single, 3,000$–5,500$ for a double; in an inland four-star *albergaria* or *estalagem* 3,500$–5,000$ for a single and 5,000$–12,000$ for a double. For a four-star hotel overlooking the beach in a big resort you could be paying double the cost of an *albergaria* or *estalagem*. Continental breakfasts are almost always included in the price of the room.

Monte do Casal hotel

Albufeira
BOA VISTA, Rua Samora Barros. Tel: 089-52175/6
Stylish modern hotel with lovely views of the bay from big windows. Situated above the town, with its own pool.
ROCAMAR, Rua Jacinto D'Ayet. Tel: 089-52611
Three-star hotel in quiet area a few minutes walk up from the village. Quite simple, but pretty décor. Steps down to beach.

Burgau
RESIDENCIAL CASA GRANDE, Tel: 082-65168
Faded grandeur. Very informal and quite eccentric, hence popular with artists and writers of all nationalities. Close to sea.

Faro and Surroundings
CASA DE LUMENA, Praça Alexandre Herculano, 27. Tel: 089-801990
Congenial three-star pension occupying old house on a central square. Antique furnishings, restaurant, bar.
EVA, Avenida da República. Tel: 089-24054
Far from inspiring eight-floor block but occupies prime location overlooking port and sea. Roof top pool, disco, top floor restaurant.
MONTE DO CASAL, Cerro do Lobo, Estoi. Tel: 089-91503
Small and exclusive, run by an English couple. Very quiet setting with lovely gardens, pool and fine views. Meals in a converted coach house or on the pool-side terrace. Twelve rooms, including some suites.
QUINTA DE BENATRITE, Santa Bárbara de Nexe, (P.O. Box 17). Tel: 089-90450
Exclusive English owned and run farmhouse, which keeps a very low profile. Member of 'The Manor Houses of Portugal' and aimed at the discriminating traveller. Well off the beaten track in quiet unspoilt countryside (you won'

find it, but you will be met). Sympathetically restored and decorated, with outstanding collection of paintings and blend of Portuguese/English antiques. Gourmet cuisine with set meals. Gardens with pool and English thoroughbreds. Only three double rooms, so advance reservations essential. Not cheap but prices well below the equivalent in the UK.

LA RÉSERVE. Santa Bárbara de Nexe. Tel: 089-90474

Part of the *Relais et Chateaux* group, hence luxurious and very pricey (B&B for two 22,000$ to 36,000$). Set in extensive grounds, 10km from Faro. Modern apartments, all with living room, air-conditioning, TV, veranda and south sea view. Large pool and tennis court. International cuisine, but mainly French.

Lagos

HOTEL DE LAGOS, 1 Rua Nova da Aldeia. Tel: 082-62011

Innovative building a few minutes' walk up from the town centre. Spacious rooms, marble hallways, fine views; free transport to Meia Praia and hotel beach club.

ALBERGARIA CASA DE SÃO GONÇALO, 73 Rua Cândido dos Reis, 8600 Lagos. Tel: 082-62171

Charming four-star *albergaria*, converted from an old town house. Full of antiques and character. Every bedroom is different. Gem of a patio where breakfast is served. Closed during the winter months.

Monchique

ALBERGARIA DO LAGEADO, Caldas de Monchique. Tel: 082-92616

Comfortable and reasonably priced for this popular spot in the Serra de Monchique. Spotless rooms, tiled floors, restaurant and pool. Sits amidst luxuriant vegetation.

ESTALAGEM ABRIGO DA MONTANHA, Estrada de Fóia. Tel: 082-92131

Delightful restaurant with rooms on mountainside; sweeping views over hills and valleys to coast. Very peaceful with only five rooms and three suites. Prices range from 6,000$–12,000$ for twin with breakfast. Half board rates available. Good Portuguese cooking. Summer meals on panoramic terrace.

MONS CICUS, Estrada de Fóia. Tel: 082-92650

Four-star *estalagem* on mountainside with swimming pools, tennis courts, sauna, bars, restaurant, country club, spacious rooms and superb views.

Penina

PENINA GOLF AND RESORT HOTEL. Tel: 082-415415

Ranks among the most luxurious hotels of the Algarve. Set in own 146ha (360-acre) estate, with Olympic-size pool, riding, sauna, shops and immaculate gardens. Free golf for residents.

Praia da Rocha

BELA VISTA. Tel: 082-24055

Fine old cliff top mansion, looking incongruous among modern blocks. One of the first hotels of the Algarve, built well before the advent of tourism. Traditional décor with fine wood panelling and tiles. The beach lies below.

Sagres

POUSADA DO INFANTE. Tel: 082-64222

Civilised state run hotel on cliff tops with views across coast to the fortress of Sagres. Marine and Henry the Navigator themes in public rooms. Attractive restaurant serving Portuguese cuisine. Garden with lush lawn, pool and

Bela Vista Hotel

tennis. All rooms have sea views. Ask for one with balcony (no extra cost).
DOM HENRIQUE, Sítio da Mareta. Tel: 082-64133
Charming four-star *residencial* on square with sea views. Neighbouring bar can be noisy.

Salema
ESTALAGEM INFANTE DO MAR, Praia de Salema. Tel: 082-65137
Attractive low lying hotel up from beach with cool whitewashed walls and tiled floors. All rooms with balcony and sea views. Pool, restaurant.
PENSÃO MARE, Praia da Salema. Tel: 082-65165
Modern, reasonably priced and congenial B&B close to the beach.

São Brás de Alportel
POUSADA DE SAO BRAS. Tel: 089-42305
1940s state run *pousada* on hill 2kms north of São Brás. Lovely views from terrace and some rooms, but could do with a face-lift in parts. Variable Portuguese cuisine. Good breakfasts. Wood burning fires in winter.

Tavira
DO CASTELO, Rua Liberdade 4. Tel: 081-23942
Central, friendly pension almost opposite the tourist office. Comfortable, modern rooms but specify a quiet one at the back.

Vale de Lobo
DONA FILIPA. Tel: 089-94141
Height of luxury and ostentation, next to the golf course.

Camping
Camping on the beach is strictly forbidden. For details on officials sites ask at any Portuguese tourist office. The Portugal Camping leaflet has information on 15 official sites in the Algarve, from one to three stars. On a well equipped three-star site, with restaurant, pool, tennis, etc, expect to pay around 1,200$ for two including tent and car in high season.

GETTING ACQUAINTED

Information Sources
The following resorts and towns have their own tourist information offices: Albufeira, Armação de Pera, Faro, Lagos, Loulé, Olhão, Portimão, Carvoeiro, Quarteira, Silves, Tavira, Vila Real de Santo António. Free leaflets are available with maps of the resorts and information on the sights to see. Look out for the *Discover* magazines for practical information on the different regions of the Algarve and the monthly *Algarve Gazette* with its sections on sightseeing and events along with general features on such subjects as fashion, golf, local news and ads galore for real estate. Both are distributed free. The *Algarve Magazine* at 400$ is glossy and fairly up market with features on art, travel, fashion, and luxury homes in the Algarve. The *Algarve News*, a tabloid newspaper distributed free, is surprisingly informative for a local rag. It covers both local and national news and gives useful information about what's on.

About half the TV shows are American or English and locals glued to soaps in cafés are a familiar sight. Both a national and regional channel show English language films in the original versions.

Algarve radio stations broadcast news bulletins and musical programmes in English. On short wave you can tune into international programmes from Europe and Voice of America.

The address of the Portuguese National Tourist Office in London is New Bond Street House, 1–5 New Bond Street, London W1Y ONP, Tel: (071) 4933873.

Tipping

Although restaurant bills normally include service it is quite common to leave a bit extra, particularly if you think the service warrants it. Hotel bills include service but doormen will appreciate a few *escudos.* If you knock on the door of the local priest to see a church, or the sacristan to go up a tower, it is usual to leave something for the upkeep of the church. A taxi driver will be delighted with a tip but won't necessarily expect one.

Business Hours

Banks are open either Monday to Friday 8.30am to 3pm or 8.30am to 11.45pm and 1pm to 2.45pm.

Shops are open Monday to Friday 9am to 1pm and 3pm to 6 or 7pm, Saturday 9am to 1pm. Markets are held from 8am to 1pm Monday to Saturday.

Public Holidays

The following days are observed as official public holidays:

New Year's Day	1 January
National Day	25 April
Labour Day	1 May
Camoens' Day	10 June
Assumption	15 August
Republic Day	5 October
All Saints' Day	1 November
Restoration Day	
(Day of Independence)	1 December
Immaculate Conception	8 December
Christmas Day	25 December

Moveable dates are Carnival, Good Friday, Easter Sunday and Corpus Christi.

HEALTH & EMERGENCIES

Tap water is not always potable. To be safe keep to bottled water, sold everywhere. Ask for *agua mineral,* either *com gas* (fizzy) or *sem gas* (still). Monchique is the local spa. Take it from the springs or drink it ready bottled.

Emergencies

Dial 115 for police, fire or ambulance.

Hospitals

The hospitals at Faro (089 22011) and Portimão (082 22132) both have a 24hr casualty department. For less urgent cases there are local hospitals at Lagos, Monchique, Lagoa, Albufeira, Loulé, São Brás de Alportel, Olhão, Tavira, Vila Real de Santo António and a British Hospital in Lisbon.

The tourist-targeted *Discover* magazines print the telephone numbers of local hospitals and English or English-speaking doctors and dentists. Pharmacies are normally open 9am to 1pm, 3pm to 7pm and work on a rotating basis after hours. The address of the open pharmacy will be listed on all pharmacy doors.

Crime

Portugal is still one of the safest countries in Europe and you are unlikely to ever come across violent crime in the Algarve. But there are increasing reports of bag snatching and car thefts, particularly from hired cars in the summer months. The thieves (often from Lisbon or Spain) sometimes work in pairs with two cars and a walkie-talkie device. Never leave valuables in the car and make sure any articles you do have are locked in the back out of sight. When you hire the car ensure that it has a proper boot or back shelf to hide the contents.

COMMUNICATIONS

Telephone

Avoid public pay phone boxes if you can. The coin boxes often need emptying and you can't get through. Instead, buy a prepaid credit card, available from post offices, some shops and cafés. They come in units of 50$ and 120$. Along the coast over half of the public booths now accept them. Alternatively,

telephone from a post office, a simple procedure whereby you ask for a booth (they will give you a line), speak for as long as you like and pay at the end of the call. You can also call from a *minimercado* or café displaying the registered CCT sign—cheaper than calling from an ordinary café. The most expensive surcharges of all are those levied by hotels.

If you are calling locally remember there are three local codes: 081 (Vila Real de Santo António and Tavira), 089 (Olhão, Faro and Albufeira) and 082 (Armação de Pera, Portimão and Lagos). If you are calling Europe, dial 00 for an international line followed by the country area codes (omitting the 0). Outside Europe dial 097, followed by the country and area code. For the international operator call 098 for Europe, 0642 for elsewhere.

Post

Opening hours of post offices vary. In large towns and resorts the hours are 8.30 or 9am to 6 or 6.30pm from Monday to Friday; 9am to 12.30pm on Saturday. Elsewhere they are closed at lunch time and on Saturday.

Mail can be collected from any post office provided it is clearly marked *Posta Restante*. You will need your passport as proof of identification. The charge is 29$. Stamps for letters under 20g cost 29$ for Portugal and Spain, 60$ for EEC countries, 65$ other European countries and 87$ outside Europe.

SPECIAL INFORMATION

The People

The Portuguese are generally good-natured, civil, relaxed and obliging. Not as loud or flamboyant as the Spanish and Italians, they are warmer in character than natives of northern climes and full of generosity. As a race they are very nationalistic. If you don't want to offend, try to avoid criticism of the country and its people. As for habits, handshaking is *de rigeur* and stretching in public if frowned upon.

The Language

Knowledge of Spanish or French helps you understand written Portuguese but the pronunciation, with its elusive nasal intonations and Eastern European sounding inflections, is a devil to understand. Nasal vowels, ie those with a tilde mark such as *ã* or *õ* or a vowel followed by *m* or *n* in certain positions, are the biggest problems as far as English speakers are concerned.

On the coast English is widely spoken, but north of the EN125 you are likely to need at least a smattering of Portuguese. Mastering even a few key words is invaluable.

Numbers

One	**Eleven**	**Thirty**
um, uma	Onze	Trinta
Two	**Twelve**	**Forty**
dois, duas	Doze	Quarenta
Three	**Thirteen**	**Fifty**
Trés	Treze	Cinquenta
Four	**Fourteen**	**Sixty**
Quatro	Catorze	Sessenta
Five	**Fifteen**	**Seventy**
Cinco	Quinze	Setenta
Six	**Sixteen**	**Eighty**
Seis	Dezasseis	Oitenta
Seven	**Seventeen**	**Ninety**
Sete	Dezassete	Noventa

Eight	Eighteen	100
Oito	Dezoito	Cem/Cento
Nine	Nineteen	1,000
Nove	Dezanove	Mil
Ten	Twenty	
Dez	Vinte	

Days of the Week
Sunday	Domingo
Monday	Segunda-feira
Tuesday	Terça-feira
Wednesday	Quarta-feira
Thursday	Quinta-feira
Friday	Sexta-feira
Saturday	Sábado

Questions
Where is..?	Onde é..?
When..?	Quando..?
How much does it cost?	
	Quanto custa?
Is there..?	Ha..?
Do you have..?	Tem..?
At what time..?	A que horas..?
Do you have a room?	
	Tem um quarto livre?

Essentials
Good morning	Bom dia
Good afternoon	Boa tarde
Good evening	Boa tarde/Boa noite
Good-night	Boa noite
Hello	Olá
Goodbye	Adeus
Please	Por Favor
Thank you	Obrigado
	(spoken by a male)
	Obrigada
	(spoken by a female)
Thank you very much	
	Muito Obrigado/a
Do you speak English?	
	Fala inglês?
I don't speak Portuguese	
	Nao falo portugues
I don't understand	
	Nao compreendo
Yes	Sim
No	Nao

USEFUL ADDRESSES & NUMBERS

BRITISH CONSULATE: Rua da Santa Isabel, Portimão, Tel: 082-23071/27057 and Rua General Humberto Delgardo 4, Vila Real de Santo António, Tel: 081-43729/43123.
US EMBASSY in Lisbon: Av das Forcas Armadas, Tel: 01-725600.
FARO AIRPORT: Tel: 089-818281–4.
FLIGHT ENQUIRIES: Tel: 089-818982.
TAP INFORMATION: Tel: 089-818539.
BRITISH AIRWAYS: Tel: 089-818320.

FURTHER READING

Good book stores are thin on the ground in the Algarve and you are best off buying reading matter before you go. Books written specifically on the Algarve are limited to pocket guides which concentrate primarily on the coast. Even on the whole of Portugal there is not a great deal of choice and much of the material is either out of print or out of date.

Portugal—General Guide Books
Insight Guide: Portugal. Apa Publications, Singapore, 1990.
Michelin Portugal and Madeira, Green Series—for general background and sightseeing.
Michelin España Portugal, Red Series—for hotels and restaurants.
Blue Guide, Portugal—In-depth coverage of all aspects of the country

Travel
They Went to Portugal, Rose Macaulay, Penguin. Entertaining account of British travellers to Portugal, from the early crusaders to 19th-century Romantic travellers.

History
A New History of Portugal, H V Livermore, Cambridge University Press, 1976. Not so new now, but very comprehensive, and readable.

Prince Henry the Navigator John Ure, Constable, 1977. Detailed account of the man who initiated the great era of discovery.

Portugal, Sarah Bradford, Thames & Hudson, 1973. Interesting account of the nation and the people, from the maritime era to the early 1970s.

Literature

The Lusiads, Luis de Camoes. Epic poem (translated) recounting the historical exploits of the Portuguese and the voyage of Vasco da Gama.

Gastronomy

Portuguese Food, Carol Wright, Dent.
The Wines of Portugal, Jan Read, Faber.

CREDITS

Photography	**Stuart Abraham** *and*
Pages: 14, 78	**Bill Wassman**
3, 26, 28/29, 81, 88, 92, 93, 95	**Tony Arruza**
Cartography	**Kaj Berndtson & Associates**
Directed by	**Hans Höfer**
Design concept by	**V. Barl**
Cover design	**Klaus Geisler**
Editorial director	**Christopher Catling**

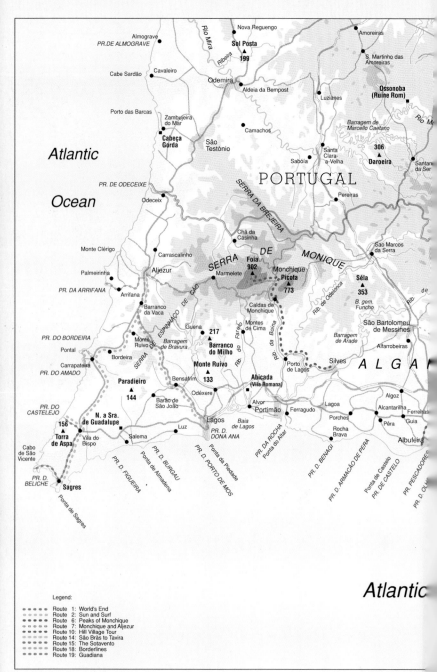

Legend:

- ● ● ● ● Route 1: World's End
- ○ ○ ○ ○ Route 2: Sun and Surf
- ● ● ● ● Route 6: Peaks of Monchique
- ○ ○ ○ ○ Route 7: Monchique and Aljezur
- ● ● ● ● Route 10: Hill Village Tour
- ● ● ● ● Route 14: São Brás to Tavira
- ● ● ● ● Route 15: The Sotavento
- ● ● ● ● Route 18: Borderlines
- ● ● ● ● Route 19: Guadiana